addicted to hurry

addicted
to hurry

SPIRITUAL strategies
for slowing down

Kirk Byron Jones

Judson Press ■ Valley Forge

Addicted to Hurry:
SPIRITUAL Strategies for Slowing Down

© 2003 by Kirk Byron Jones
Published by Judson Press, Valley Forge, PA 19482-0851
All rights reserved.

Judson Press has made every effort to document all quotes. In the event of a question arising from the use of a quote, we sincerely regret any error made and will be pleased to make the necessary correction in future printings and editions of this book.

Bible quotations in this volume are from the New Revised Standard Version of the Bible, copyright © 1989 by the Division of Christian Education of the National Council of Churches of Christ in the United States of America. Used by permission. All rights reserved.

ISBN: 0-7394-3949-9

Printed in the U.S.A.

To Mary Brown-Jones,
my marvelous merry-making spouse,
affectionately known to family and friends as
"Bunnie." Thank you for your fun and faithfulness.

contents

acknowledgments

GREAT GRATITUDE TO GOD FOR IT ALL!

I am grateful to Linda Peavy and the Judson Press family for your steadfast commitment to this project in the rain of challenge and change. I want to especially thank Randy Frame for earlier on pushing me to make *Addicted to Hurry* more practically meaningful. I salute, as well, Victoria McGoey, a person of expansive competence and grace. A smile of gratitude to Wendy Ronga for a compelling cover.

Shari Smothers, a kindred spirit from New Orleans and an extraordinary poet, took the time to read the words, and just as importantly, to listen to the sounds and pauses of the manuscript. Thank you, Shari.

If you were with me as I write this now, you would see that I am surrounded by books, music CDs, and other unsung stuff (don't underestimate the stuff of life). This book is supported by a host of literary, musical, and other assorted inspirations and dialogical partners. For both conscious and unconscious interaction, I am grateful.

The offering of my thoughts in these pages has been enhanced by hundreds of persons who have dialoged with me in seminars and other settings around the country. Your questions and suggestions have pushed me to greater clarity of understanding and expression. Thank you all.

For sure, I thank five gifts of personhood who support my work, play, and overall silliness: Bunnie, my wife to whom this book is dedicated, and Jasmine, Jared, Joya, and Jovonna. Together, we are the Joneses at 39 Stoughton Street, Randolph, Massachusetts.

Dear family, thank you for noticing my noticing you.

They heard the sound of the L<small>ORD</small> *God walking*
in the garden at the time of the evening breeze.

—Genesis 3:8

introduction

The Need for Speed

FAST IS FUN! REMEMBER THE RUNNING GAMES YOU played as a child, like hide and seek, and those games that demanded quick movement, like dodge ball? I especially enjoyed football and its variations. My brothers, Fred, Wayne, and Vincent, and I used to play "running through." The four of us would stand in the grass in the lot next to our house. One of us would then throw a football high into the air. The person who caught the ball was obliged to run with it until he was caught or fell to the ground of utter fatigue. I smile as I write about it. Running was a vital dimension of my childhood and maybe yours too. I can still hear Cousin Florida yelling at my playground football league games, "Run, Kirk, run!"

The pleasure power of speed is not limited to the days of youth. For example, I enjoy the fast rhythms of classic jazz bebop music by artists such as Charlie Parker and Dizzy Gillespie. I also enjoy computer gaming, a hobby enhanced by the presence of a fast graphics card, which allows games to operate more smoothly.

As we grow, we realize that fast is not just fun but necessary. How many times in the past few months have you swerved to the side to allow a police car, fire truck, or ambulance swift passage?

Haste is not just an important tool for emergency workers but also for many others, from the janitor who has a set number of offices to clean by a certain time to the diplomat working to prevent international conflict before time is up. In your job, how many instances can you think of in which haste helps you to fulfill your responsibility? I think we all would agree that the speed technology encased in computers, copiers, cell phones, and faxes has helped to make us more efficient and productive.

In my African American, Baptist worship tradition, fast can be a mighty worship force. I have in mind—and some of you know exactly what I am talking about—instances when a moving song concludes, only to have a "sanctified P.S." added. Suddenly the organist and accompanying musicians will launch a fast, rhythmic praise beat, and the whole church explodes in ecstatic clapping, dancing, and shouting. This is high-octane worship! You either join in as best you can or get out of the way.

If fast is fun, necessary, productive, and even sacred, what's the problem with speed? What's wrong with hurry?

An Unhealthy Addiction

I had purchased a breakfast meal from a world-famous fast-food franchise. As I sat eating and welcoming the morning, I looked at the bag that I had not crumbled and tossed into the trash. It was still there standing before me. That's when I saw it, a large speedometer on the bag with the following designations: "fast," "really fast," "really, really fast," and at the end, the franchise's golden arches with a drive-thru sign underneath that I assumed stood for "really, really, really fast." Where do you think the indicator was on this marketing image designed to communicate speed of service? One notch *past* really, really fast. The message communicated to the masses is all too clear: "We are presently moving at a blazing speed, and we are striving to be even faster."

For a moment, imagine that you are present at the marketing meeting in which this idea is first being discussed. Why is this idea being offered? How do others present respond to it? Why do people think it's going to be effective? What are the chances of this concept making the journey from the boardroom to the bag with, quite possibly, little opposition? The chances are very good, aren't they? Why? Marketing personnel get paid to know the market inside and out, and they know that through and through ours is a culture addicted to speed. Marketing knows that many people will consciously and unconsciously appreciate the message of speedy service. Marketing knows that one of life's greatest common denominators across cultural, gender, and age lines is hurry. Hurry is not just a part of life; hurry *is* life.

When hurry becomes a chronic condition, when we run even when there is no reason to, when we rush while performing even the most mundane tasks, it may be said that we have become addicted to hurry. Thousands of us are addicted to hurry whether we admit it or not. *Denial* is not a river in Egypt.

Denying the addiction to hurry involves denying the costs of the addiction. As long as we are blind to the ways chronic hurry harms us physically, emotionally, socially, and spiritually, we can keep on running even when we are bone tired. As we face up to the unnecessary and unacceptable sacrifices that result from living as though we were being chased, we develop the tenacious intent needed to create a more humane, peaceful, and sustainable pace for ourselves and our world.

Hurry is often cited as a contributing factor in tragedies resulting in accidents and loss of life. How many car accidents happen each year due to speeding? Sometimes cars aren't involved. Just a few days ago a twenty-one-year-old woman was killed in Massachusetts trying to board a train. She misjudged the distance of an oncoming train as she fixed on obeying the command of family members who had gone before her and told her to "hurry up." Even when hurry is not so directly linked to fatalities, it is a suspected culprit. Such was the case a few years ago when a man left his child in a locked, hot automobile all day long. He thought he had dropped her off at the nursery. He did not notice his tragic error until he went to the nursery to pick up his child.

Tragedies can wake us up to the monumental costs of hurry in an instant. They can also cause us to think more deeply about hidden ways hurry harms us on a daily basis. As I write this on October 9, 2002, there is a sniper loose in the Washington, D.C., area. This person has killed seven persons and wounded two others. The latest victim is a thirteen-year-old boy who was getting out of his mother's vehicle at school. Residents, especially children and parents, are filled with anxiety and fear. One picture I saw online showed a mother lovingly clutching her visibly distraught son. As I observed the picture, I grieved for the violent slaughter of the innocent and for our need for tragedies to remind us how precious our children are. Unintentionally but sadly, we go about our frenzied multitasking and leave children to accept our complete absence or our divided attention when we are present. There is a grave unsung crisis in the land: *being too hurried to give serious attention to our children between crises.*

An Overview

My first objective in this book is to show how chronic speed is constantly diminishing our lives relationally, emotionally, and spiritually. Second, I want to suggest to you an anti-rushing, pro-relishing way of living that can help you to stop rushing and to start savoring life more. Seeds for both objectives were planted in my first book, *Rest in the Storm: Self-Care Strategies for Clergy and Other Caregivers.* Many insights presented in this book were nurtured in discussions surrounding that initial attempt to address the malady of overdriven, overcommitted living in service to a laudable cause. Thomas Merton's characterization of such living as a form of violence deserves to be voiced again: "There is a pervasive form of contemporary violence ... [and that is] activism and overwork. The rush and pressure of modern life are a form, perhaps the most common form, of its innate violence."

This book is divided into two sections: diagnosis and prescription. I begin by discussing our cultural addiction to speed. Some findings from sociologists may surprise you. In chapter 2, I identify various reasons for our running. In chapters 3 through 5, I present what I believe are the three deeper forces behind living in a hurry: fear of hurt, fear of ourselves, and fear of God. At the end of this diagnosis section, I want you to believe that the second worst response to hurry is making light of it. The worst response is accepting it. We must come to accept something else about chronic hurry: Hurry is not an innocent and inevitable consequence of modern life. Chronic hurry is a serious malady of mind, heart, and soul putting at risk our relationship with God, each other, and ourselves.

The theologian Richard J. Mouw writes in an article entitled "Humility, Hope, and the Divine Slowness" that "we have God's permission to take our time." Can we imagine that this statement is true, and if so, can we give ourselves the same permission?

Chapter 6 shifts our focus from problem to solution. In this remedy section, I will challenge you to envision an achievable alternative to hurry: cultivating your own sacred, savoring pace. I will offer my testimony of how a new appreciation for the sacred pace of Jesus and an Alaskan vacation experience inspired me to a savoring pace way of life. Most importantly, chapters 6 through 10 will teach you how to live at a sacred savoring pace: to see more clearly, listen more carefully, and think more deeply. Savoring pace is about taking the time to notice more. While we cannot notice everything, *believing that everything is worth noticing* can dynamically enliven life.

Along the way, you will learn that savoring pace is not simply about slowing down. Jesus did not promise life in slow motion (sustained slowness is not very compelling); he promised life more abundantly. While slowing down is helpful, beating hurry addiction is more than a matter of merely slowing down. Remember, there are things about hurry that we enjoy. Because of this, many of us will subconsciously view slowing down as an irritant at best and a threat at worst. We don't want to just slow down. Slowing down is too passive and uninspiring an enterprise; we are wired for more. A viable alternative to hurry must yield joys and fulfillments that rival those of hurry.

Learning to live at a savoring pace is about slowing down and intentionally attending to *the showing in the slowing*. Savoring pace is slowness for enrichment's sake. You cannot rush and relish at the same time. Some of the most striking beauty this world has to offer is missed in the rush. As I edit this manuscript, there is a winter wonderland outside. Tree limbs are outlined with two-inch-thick snow, and the sun is doing more sightseeing than thawing in the cold Thanksgiving morning.

Savoring or relishing life is a sacred practice. When it comes to articulating the most enduring relationship of all, David, the biblical poet/king, speaks in savoring terms: "Taste and see that the Lord is good." In the prevailing haste of our existence, we must discover what it means to taste and see God, and to taste and see God's extravagant gift of life. Savoring pace is not just a timely speed corrective; it is a compelling sacred calling. The chapters on the savoring pace alternative are based on this presumption: *Each of us has the power to imagine, create, and practice a healthier, holier lifestyle free from chronic hurry.*

Finally, a word of caution. Even if you indulge the temptation to read the remedy section first, I implore you to go back at some point and read about why we run. A deeper understanding of the reasons behind our racing may inspire the necessary deeper changes in the way we think and act regarding hurry. This book is not about simple adjustment; it is about vigilant change. To that end, each chapter contains practical application questions and exercises that will help make this book a positive transformative experience.

1

the idolatry of speed

"*Speed is God, and time is the Devil.*"
—David Hancock, chief of Hitachi
Corporation's portable computer division,
quoted in *Faster* by James Gleick

"*One day, when I timed an annoying (computer) delay
and found that it constituted all of ten seconds, I had
what I would call a 'monk moment,' a quick slap that
told me,* Pay attention—watch yourself. *I had let
technology and its attendant idol, efficiency, make a
fool of me.*"
—Kathleen Norris

THE RENOWNED PREACHER REV. BARBARA BROWN
Taylor once began a sermon on idols by sharing a personal
experience. She was driving toward her home one night
when she saw a large steer outside a fence. She lived next
door to a cattle rancher, so she thought to contact him as

soon as possible. On her way to the ranch, she noticed the huge, perfectly proportioned animal once again. Amazingly, its posture was exactly the same as before. She focused her eyes in the darkness of night and smiled to herself. The large animal had not changed position because it could not. She was, in fact, looking at a huge, gorgeous, lifelike statue.

Idols, in whatever shape or form, grab our attention, and if we are not careful, our ultimate loyalty. Once they have our attention in this way, idols—things we make—pull a treacherous switch: they begin making us. The third danger of idols is that we usually never own up to how dangerous they really are. The best idols remain cloaked in the garments of innocent acceptableness. By these criteria, hurry may be seen as one of our culture's most dangerous and pernicious idols.

The Omnipresence of Speed

Speed is all around us via technology, communication, and transportation. There is no question that life has been enhanced in numerous ways through speeding up things. What we may question is the prevalence of speed in dimensions of life that are not so obvious and in ways that are not so beneficial. Take, for instance, language. How many everyday expressions can you think of that are used to promote speed in some way or another? Here are a few:

I am going as fast as I can
speedy recovery
hurry up
mad dash
get a move on
ASAP

the sooner, the better
step on it
shake a leg
get cracking
I've got to run
I don't have much time
wait a minute
just a second
right away
how soon can I expect it?
running late
running scared
run down
running out of time
grab a bite
on the run
it'll only take a minute

In addition, we have developed a mini-dictionary of compound words that start with "instant," "fast," and "express." How many such words can you come up with?

Pick a day to note how many of these fast phrases you say and hear. You'll be surprised. When I purchased a car recently, I was surprised to notice many cars, painted the exact same color, on the road. Similarly, when you start listening for them, you'll notice that *fast phrases* are all around us, all the time.

Do you remember the fast-food bag I talked about in the introduction? When it comes to speed and language it is not just what we say to each other but what the marketing boom box says to us from the time we get up to the time we go to bed. To my left is a reference book for one of the most popular desktop information management programs. The appeal to speed is unmistakably clear regarding the marketing of this and other products offered by this mega—and for many of us indispensable—software provider. The title of the manual on my desk is "At a Glance: The Right Answers, Right Now." Turn to the back of the manual, and you are introduced to products and the following accompanying phrases:

Keep fast answers in your pocket!

Master [the name of the product] in a hurry!

Stay in the running for maximum productivity.

Step up!

My point is not to disparage any of the products; I use some of them. I do want you to notice the appeal to speed in each of the phrases. It is not an accident. Marketing departments invest massive sums of money to locate and press the right buttons inside of us. They know that speed is one of our biggest buttons, maybe our biggest. These are examples from a single company. Over the next few days, take the time to notice and even record marketing messages for other products that play on our need for speed.

Speed is a main ingredient not just of what we say but what we do. There are the obvious examples of speeding drivers, hastily moving pedestrians, and talkers who seem to pride themselves on acceleration of speech. We see and live this behavior. But the omnipresence of speed comes out in less obvious but no less significant ways. For example, one morning I was standing in the checkout line of an office supply store. There were a couple of people ahead of me, and I was in no hurry, or so I thought. As I glanced to my right I saw another store associate making his way to a register. There it was, an opening, my chance! Before I knew it, I was standing before him. I have observed this behavior in supermarkets. As soon as a new register opens, there is a sprint toward that line. It is almost as if a thermostat inside of us is set on hurry. We gravitate toward speed even when there is no reason to. How many minutes did I save in the store? Why did I need to be waited on as soon as possible, even when soon was less than a minute earlier? It is not just that speed is all around us. Something more ominous is at work: speed is inside of us. Many of us are inhabited by a speed impulse. We do well to be concerned: *Anything inside of you is not just a matter of word and deed but of heart and soul.*

The Omnipotence of Speed

It is one thing to accept speed as a necessary fact of life; it is another thing to crown speed lord of life. Stan Davis and Christopher Meyer come close to doing just that. They have even named the god of speed BLUR:

Don't think that you'll ever slow down BLUR, let alone bring it to a halt. Its constant acceleration is here to stay, and those who miss that point will miss everything. Your job as a manager, as an entrepreneur, as a consumer, and as an individual is to master BLUR, to keep the acceleration going, to keep your world changing and off balance. Stop trying to clarify it, codify it, explain it. Recognize it. Learn its new rules. You'll then be able to move at BLUR's speed—and discover that you can thrive in amazing new ways.[1]

These are dangerous assertions moving hurry from questionable fact to unchallenged faith. Speed is not only accepted but it is also applauded as a regulating ideal of life.

5

In *Speed Is Life,* Bob Davis writes about the unsurpassed sheer power of speed to influence culture, particularly in the business world:

> Speed saves lives in all fields, but in business today it is the great differentiation, an essential survival tool. We live in a world where a company is measured by its ability to accelerate everything from manufacturing to marketing, from hiring to distributing. If we can produce or process something faster, we can often do it for less money, serve our customers better, and get a jump on our competitors. For almost any business these days, speed is indeed life.[2]

Davis concludes with a remarkable observation about the primacy of speed: "I was lucky enough to have been on the front lines of the Internet revolution—a revolution that was powered by technology but driven by speed."

The Speed of Omniscience

No, the heading is not a misprint. When it comes to the other "o" word we use to comprehend the definitive features of divinity, I do not want to assert that speed is all-knowing.

I do want you to think nonjudgmentally for a moment about how fast our knowing has become. With the advent of computers and the Internet, it is possible for us to know in hours what generations before us could not even fathom. Dr. Richard Swenson observes, "A single edition of the *New York Times* contains more information than a seventeenth-century Britisher would encounter in a lifetime." That we know so much so fast is a delightful and dizzying fact of life.

There is something else about speed and knowledge that I want you to think about: the emphasis we place on having fast answers over good answers. How many game shows can you think of in which speed of response is as important, if not more important, than quality of response? On your job, do you sometimes sense that how fast you work matters more than how well you work? Are speed and competency one in the same in your employer's mind? Are they the same in yours?

Seven Serious Sacrifices

The thirty-second chapter of the Book of Exodus, the text from which Dr. Taylor drew her sermon, is very dramatic and tragic. In the absence of Moses and the God they had come to know through Moses, the people cry out for another god. They need something to fill the deepening void of their temporarily departed—though they do not know it is temporary—spiritual leader. To appease their mounting anxiety, Aaron, Moses' brother, creates a god figure, a golden calf. This sets off a terrible chain reaction. God is filled with wrath which "burn[s] hot." God's wrath is transferred to Moses, who breaks "the work of God," "the writing of God engraved on the tablets," by violently tossing them to the foot of the mountain. Moses destroys the golden calf and makes the people drink its remains. Finally, three thousand brothers, friends, and neighbors are killed by their brothers, friends, and neighbors. All of this happens as a result of the ultimate loyalty confusion: treating something that is not God as if it were God. Idolatry, no matter how innocent and unintended, leads to unnecessary losses and sacrifices.

We suffer many unnecessary sacrifices as a result of our addiction to speed, our speed idolatry. On the scale of life's most important matters, some of these are minor, such as

7

running off and forgetting your freshly brewed tea on the kitchen counter. (This is actually a second concession to speed. The first is not observing the time to savor your morning brew at home.) Some matters are not minor. I have in mind seven serious unnecessary sacrifices because of our addiction to speed: *patience, judgment, depth, joy, dialogue, personhood, and spirituality.*

Patience

David Baily Harned begins his wonderful book, *Patience: How We Wait Upon the World,* as follows:

> Less than forty years ago a dictionary of Christian ethics was published by the Press of one of the church's major and most literate denominations. It was edited by an eminent theologian and its eighty contributors from various religious communities were drawn equally from both sides of the Atlantic. The dictionary contained entries on pessimism, pleasure, polygamy, prostitution, and propaganda, but there was no listing for patience.[3]

In our pushing and rushing, many of us have no listing, leave no place, for patience. This is an especially serious indictment for Christians. While speed is not listed as one of the "fruits of the Spirit" in Galatians 5:22, patience is.

Family communication is an area often lacking patience. Contrary winds of bitterness and strife would blow less often if we took a few moments longer to listen to each other. Nowhere is looking without seeing and hearing without listening more widespread than in the home. Proximity breeds familiarity; familiarity breeds assumption; assumption breeds impatience. We end up evidencing little patience for the people and concerns that are of utmost importance to us.

Outside the home, patience is equally as important. Patience is a necessary tool for living in a world characterized by increasing complexity and paradox. Without patience, despair and cynicism become our most preferred options. Patience—alert waiting—readies us for creative breakthrough and imaginative problem solving.

Judgment

Chronic speed diminishes our capacity to notice and target dangerous behavior. In *Married to the Job*, psychotherapist Ilenc Philipson offers testimony after testimony of persons who allowed work to run roughshod over other commitments, especially family. While agreeing with other social scientists that widespread consumerism is behind much of our overworking, Philipson argues that emotional need is as strong an influence. Overcommitment to a company is easier when we perceive such work evoking joy, social connection, and a sense of self-worth inside of us.

While hurry may have nothing to do with how overwork begins, I believe it does have something to do with how it is sustained. One of the ways to avoid constructive critique about overwork, or any unhealthy behavior, is to be too hurried to hear criticism or to notice physical warning signals. Hurry and busyness are effective evasive strategies. What we do not allow ourselves to hear, for the moment at least, is not real and does not matter. This may be termed the "Ain't no stopping me now, I'm on the move" syndrome.

When our critical judgment is impaired, we are unable to see the larger array of options before us. Just before writing this, I noticed something in the field of trees across the street from our home. It is something that I would not have noticed with a quick glance. Because I was sitting and staring, I noticed leaves floating down from the trees in the chilled October morning air. First one, then another, and so it continued, slowly and serenely. This was a noteworthy moment for me. Having lived in the Northeast for twelve years now, I am thrilled by the beautiful foliage that occurs at this time of year. (I am admittedly not quite as excited about the raking chores that follow.) I am used to observing the changing colors of the leaves and collecting them from the ground before the first snow of winter. Watching them float from the trees, however, was a new blessing bequeathed to me by the unsung motions of sitting and staring.

How much of our decision making is hampered by fast thinking? We are so used to thinking quickly that we do not assess the harm of speeded-up judgments. Rushed thinking usually severely restricts our ability to envision viable options. How many times have we made poor decisions because we did not take the time to sit and stare at a matter? Our haste did not allow time for us to see what can be seen only through patient consideration. Often the consequences of a poor decision can be discerned in advance, through patient pondering beforehand. Some mistakes are unavoidable; others are manufactured by hasty decision making.

Depth

George Duke, premiere musician and producer, explained how he came to prioritize depth of musical expression over dexterity, playing a lot of notes as nimbly as possible: "I got that from John Coltrane. As a kid, I snuck over to the *Jazz Workshop* in San Francisco. And some sax player was playing a lot of notes, man. I was astonished, but then 'Trane' came up to solo and played one note, and there was so much force and direction in that one note. I said, 'When I can do that, I'll know I've arrived.' "[4]

Speed has its moments, and sometimes those are crucial, life-saving moments. But whereas speed is salvation in some instances, it is damnation in others. One of the great hallmarks of Christian theology is eternal life, life after death. Rushing is a way of diminishing the depth of something else that should matter to us: life before death.

Joy

Joy, another fruit of the Spirit, is a frequent casualty of hurry. Ironically, we have duped ourselves into believing that hurry is a way toward joy. For example, a popular Boston radio station repeats this phrase throughout the day: "We'll help your work day fly by." I understand the marketing appeal. Many people are generally dissatisfied with their employment. Music will help make the work day go by, the faster the better. However, I wonder how much work dissatisfaction is aggravated rather than appeased by such musically induced swiftness. What if taking things more slowly allowed us to create new challenge, delight, and meaning for work grown stale? Moreover, in our desire for work to fly by, we unwittingly miss savoring those sacred moments when the line between work and play becomes blurred.

In our rushing, we neglect meaningful delights. One of the best beginnings to any book I have ever read is found in

John Stilgoe's *Outside Lies Magic: Regaining History and Awareness in Everyday Places.* Here is his memorable plea to recover one of the lost simple joys of life: exploration.

> GET OUT NOW. Not just outside, but beyond the trap of the programmed electronic age so gently closing around so many people at the end of our century. Go outside, move deliberately, then relax, slow down, look around. Do not jog. Do not run. Forget about blood pressure and arthritis, cardiovascular rejuvenation and weight reduction. Instead pay attention to everything that abuts the rural road, the city street, the suburban boulevard. Walk, Stroll, Saunter. Ride a bike, and coast along a lot. Explore.[5]

There is yet another kind of joy we miss out on in our scurrying about, the joy of contentment. Nowhere is this more evident than during the end-of-the-year holiday season. We soil the season with unhindered consumerism that seems to get worse every year. Think about if you have ever begun a prayer in the following fashion: "God, thank you. For in this moment I have a profoundly satisfying sense of having all that I truly need."

Dialogue

Dialogue, like patience, is dangerously underrated. Dialogue is ongoing conversation that involves participants placing as much emphasis on listening as they do on speaking. Many modern maladies, from domestic violence to international conflict, are directly linked to the absence of dialogue. Dialogue leads to familiarity, which melts away fear. Hurry is a way of absenting ourselves from dialogue and consequently holding fast to our fears.

Dialogue with others is not the only casualty of hurried living. In our running from this to that, we have no time to dialogue with ourselves. Personal growth hinges on time to welcome the arrival of new questions and to ponder the deepening meaning of old ones. Self-dialogue is one of the most important conversations of all, especially at points when we are most troubled. We need time to wade through the waters of disorienting questions, exactly the kind that lead us to new awareness and insight. Often the breakthrough we need if not long for is on the other side of such rough passing.

Personhood

The recent rise in books about self-care is unnerving to some people. Some observers feel that such works are feeding the narcissistic me-ism that has historically plagued us in the United States. One of the influential books of the past twenty years, *Habits of the Heart,* challenges our overfixation with individualism. With all due respect to these legitimate critiques, many Christians have the opposite problem. They have committed living self-suicide in order to conform to prevailing unholy and unhealthy models of discipleship. I have in mind persons who lead hectic lives as an expression of their faith. They believe that chronic exhaustion is a sign of deeply committed living, that burnout is an expression of piety. Contrary to popular behavior, God does not need our exhaustion. There is nothing holy about running ourselves into the ground. There is nothing spiritual about being all things to all people as soon as possible.

Rushing is an enemy of personhood. Hurried living dupes us into believing, in the words of Dr. Richard Swenson, "that exhaustion is normal, that a listless spirit is inevitable, and that burnout is piety." These lethal beliefs are slowly sapping the vitality of millions every day. Bryan Robinson describes this perilous plight: "Our supercharged lives are stuck in fast forward and focused on the external world. We do not have an internal life. Overdoing it keeps us disconnected from ourselves, subtracts from our human value and prevents us from knowing who we are."[6]

Personhood is a blessing. Personhood is holy prior to expressing itself in vocation. *Being* is as important as *doing*. Perhaps the early church father Irenaeus puts the sacredness of personhood best: "The glory of God is a person fully alive."

Spirituality

Patience, depth, joy, dialogue, and personhood are all dimensions of spirituality. By separating it out, giving spirituality its own unique space, I mean to highlight spirituality as our wrestling with matters of the heart and soul. By spirituality, I also mean our engagement with God, who is always beyond our finest and fullest thoughts.

Though ever present, our spirituality is keenly felt in moments of absorption, awe, and awakening. By absorption, I mean those times when we are so involved in what we are doing that we lose (and loose) all sense of place and time. This is complete kinship with the now, the precious present of life. Being overcome with laughter that is not at the expense of another is a moment of overwhelming absorption for me. I am talking about laughter to the point of being bent over and almost crying. Such laughter is all-consuming, unleashing gushing joy.

By awe, I mean those "wow" moments of life when we simply don't have the words to describe what we are experiencing. Wow moments can happen in any place, anywhere, and at any time.

By awakening, I mean having a new awareness ignited inside of us that makes a difference in how we live. Awakenings can be great and small. They are never uneventful. With each awakening we feel more alive. And there is this paradoxical blessing as well: With each new awakening we feel farther away from and yet closer to home. Real awakening creates dissatisfaction with the familiar and desire for the strange. We feel drawn to experiences of absorption, awe, and awakening. These have even more potent, transformative energy when they involve our engagement with the ineffable God, the God who is much more than we can ever imagine.

Absorption, awe, awakening as they relate to God or loving Mystery comprise holy ground indeed.

Perhaps matters of ecclesiology, religion, and theology can be rushed at times with no great loss or impact. This is not the case when it comes to spirituality. Spirituality rarely involves rushing. The matters are weighted with too much fear in the best sense of the word and delight in every sense of the word. Spirituality is courted by attentiveness. Maybe this is what the clergyman had in mind when he said, "Hurry is the devil." How can we experience sacred absorption, awe, and awakening if we do not have time to pay attention? *Rushed sacredness is a hoax.*

Notes

1. Stan Davis and Christopher Meyer, *Blur: The Speed of Change in the Connected Economy* (New York: Warner Books, 1999), 2–8.

2. Bob Davis, *Speed Is Life: Street Smart Lessons from the Front Lines of Business* (New York: Doubleday, 2001).
3. David Baily Harned, *Patience: How We Wait Upon the World* (Boston: Cowley Publications, 1997), 1.
4. George Duke, *Jazzis*, November 2002, 15.
5. John Stilgoe, *Outside Lies Magic: Regaining History and Awareness in Everyday Places* (New York: Walker & Company, 1998), 1.
6. Bryan Robinson, "Breaking Our Patters of Overdoing It," *Lotus*, Anniversary 1995, 36.

Exercise: Are You Addicted to Speed?
What's Your Pace Quotient?

1. You are behind a driver who has not noticed that the light has turned green. How do you respond?
   ___ a. Give the person a moment to notice the light has changed
   ___ b. Blow your horn immediately
   ___ c. Blow your horn and express your irritation verbally

2. You are in a slow-moving grocery line with time to spare. What are you most likely to do?
   ___ a. Engage in a conversation with someone else
   ___ b. Look repeatedly at the person at the register to see how fast things are going
   ___ c. Become irritated

3. In conversing with others, how often do you interrupt them in mid-sentence?
   ___ a. Not very often
   ___ b. Some of the time
   ___ c. Very often

4. How much time during the day do you devote to prayer, pondering, meditation, and/or just taking it easy?
   ___ a. At least an hour
   ___ b. At least half an hour
   ___ c. Less than half an hour

5. Someone/thing has interrupted your planned activity. Select the word that best describes your gut feeling:
   ___ a. Interested
   ___ b. Disturbed
   ___ c. Aggravated

6. Which word best characterizes your mood at the beginning of an average day?
   ___ a. Excited
   ___ b. Burdened
   ___ c. Depressed

7. Which word best describes your emotional state at the end of an average day?
   ___ a. Contented
   ___ b. Fatigued
   ___ c. Stressed

8. When you see a rainbow, how long does it hold your attention?
   ___ a. Many minutes
   ___ b. Several seconds
   ___ c. Just a second

9. When was the last time you paid serious attention to a child?
   ___ a. Today
   ___ b. Within the past few days
   ___ c. I can't remember

10. How often do you feel joy in your work?
    ___ a. Frequently
    ___ b. Often enough
    ___ c. Are you kidding?

11. How often do you hurry one activity to get to the next activity?
    ___ a. Not often
    ___ b. Regularly
    ___ c. All the time

12. How often do you move fast when there is no reason to?
    ___ a. Never
    ___ b. Sometimes
    ___ c. I confess, I have rushed through this test

A. Review your responses.

B. Which responses do you wish were different?

C. Think of other questions that will help you gauge your present living speed.

D. Note the behaviors identified in each question. Develop one or two modifications in your behavior that will contribute to your being able to check off more (a) responses the next time you take the test, a month or two from now.

2

see why we run

"There are people who want to be everywhere at once and get nowhere."
—Carl Sandburg

DO YOU RECALL THE NURSERY RHYME "THREE BLIND Mice" and the refrain "See how they run"? In this chapter, we will observe how we run, but even more, *why* we run. You will note that most of the reasons identified are understandable, some noble even. The problem is not so much that the reasons are bad. The real problem is that the reasons are numerous, incessant, and cumulative in their impact on us. Because of so many speed cues, we are under constant, often hidden, pressure to live as soon as possible all the time. The following list is not in order of importance or prevalence. We all run for different sets of reasons. Your reason for running may not be on this list. Pay attention to what I have left out.

We run out of enthusiasm. Running is an integral part of play. If you want a nice, easy pick-me-up, watch children at recess in a schoolyard. Their running is an expression of enthusiasm and vitality. Enthused running is not limited to the days of our youth. We run to phones and mailboxes with tiptoe expectancy. We run to loved ones at airports and train and bus stations in unhindered affection. We run to engagements and events, not just out of tardiness but anticipation. Being in a hurry is holy when it comes to enthusiasm. "Enthusiasm" derives from *en theos*, which means "in God." Enthusiasm, or sacred excitement, is the sentiment expressed by Jazz saxophonist and composer Benny Golsen about the feeling shared by many of his musical friends during the 1940s and 1950s: "Oh it was so fertile, man! Every day was an adventure. We wanted to sleep fast so we could wake up and start again."[1]

We run to get things done. The faster we move, we surmise, the more we are able to do. Of course the desire to accomplish, to perform, to do, is not intrinsically evil. Indeed, it is holy. I am married to a marvelous woman who is very much a morning person. It is not unusual for her to talk about daily tasks she is looking forward to while we are still waking up. What a blessing to be able to ride toward the day with a sense of direction. Planning to do energizes us; successfully doing what we have planned fulfills us and builds in us a sense of onward surge and an overall feeling of progress in life.

We all know the real if fleeting feeling of contentment that comes in the space between tasks. Planning to do and doing are formidable positive forces of creative living. Often we run to keep up with these forces. We run because of what is running inside us. We are wired to work, to labor, and to create.

We run because the clock is running. Sometimes when I am writing I am amazed at the passage of time. I will look at the clock and see 9 A.M. I'll look what seems like a few minutes later, and I find myself staring at the noon hour. We have all asked at one time or another, "Where has the time gone?" You may experience this while reading, drawing, gardening, or performing another task that absorbs you. For some, this sense of time acceleration is not limited to specific tasks or periodic episodes. They are shrouded with a chronic sense of speeded-up time. Their unconscious response is often notching up the speed of life in order to keep up with the speed of time. Do you know persons who always seem be on the run even when they are off the work clock? Though they are off one clock, they are on another inside timer that never stops.

We run because there is so much to do. If you are a working parent of young children it is quite possible that you regularly complete the following tasks before 9 A.M.:

awaken children
observe a morning devotional
exercise
glance at e-mail
receive brief informal and/or work-related phone calls
iron clothing
prepare breakfast
shower/dress
dress children
mediate family disagreements
transport children to bus or school
travel through heavy traffic
prepare for your first meeting/project of the day

Most of the items mentioned above do not relate to children. Persons with and without children feel similar and unique pressures to move as fast as possible to accomplish necessary tasks. Is it any wonder that some people feel like they have already been to work before arriving at their jobs?

For some, haste is the obvious tool for managing the over-load of multifarious, ordinary demands of living; there is no other way to accomplish tasks that are essential to personal and familial well-being. The nature of such necessary func-tioning makes it difficult to challenge domestic hurry with-out feeling guilty and negligent. We wearily accept haste as a necessary by-product of modern, overloaded life, some-times marveling at our ability to do as well as we do, think-ing in the words of the title of a recent best seller, *I Don't Know How She [He] Does It.*

We run to acquire prized possessions. I have in mind keeping up with the latest styles and gadgets. Do you remember the frenzy surrounding the Elmo doll and the Playstation II game system a few years ago? People awoke early and stood in long lines for hours to secure items that were hugely and successfully marketed as must-haves. Certifying items as prized possessions creates a hunger and thirst for them. That hunger and thirst only intensifies with word that such items are available in limited quantities. Owning prized posses-sions boosts our sense of status and increases our sense of social acceptance. Owning prized possessions as soon as possible before the masses makes us feel like a prized pos-sessor—before the masses.

We run to catch up. If you are a list maker, the evidence for this is probably nearby. Rarely are we ever able to accom-plish the ten, twenty, or thirty tasks we set out to perform each day. The reasons are legion: interruptions, tasks taking longer to accomplish than time allotted, changes in priori-ties, personal needs. Often the first remedy we apply to falling behind schedule is speeding up. We assume that if we move faster we can somehow catch up with the workload so that by the end of the day we will have successfully crossed off everything on the list. Rarely are we able to do this, because the speed solution ends up secretly sabotaging us. Rushing produces mistakes, tensions, and frustrations, effectively throwing us off our best work rhythm and setting us even further behind. So much for catching up.

We run to avoid being late. Promptness is a value in our society, and for good reason. Familial, organizational, and social harmony depends on time plans and agreements. Though there is usually understanding and grace for extenuating circumstances, a reputation for chronic tardiness tends to strain relationships. Thus some of our running has to do with desiring to be respectful and faithful in social relationships. This impulse is commendable except when it is combined with a muted ability to discern excessive commitments. The resulting layered frustration is constant tardiness on top of, and in spite of, constant rushing. This is the thick tension we create by trying desperately to be in too many places at the same time.

We run because of our jobs. Vocationally, a running temperament may have external and internal influences. By external, I mean hurry that is caused by organizational expectation and environment. By internal, I mean the hurry that rises up out of our beliefs and desires.

If you are currently employed in a work setting where you do not feel pushed to get things done, count your blessing. There are many jobs in which salary and position are determined by policies and evaluation criteria that prioritize speed. Hurry is a built-in component of the job. Another dimension of job-enforced hurry is the organizational culture that develops out of institutional expectations. Informed by such expectations or cues, we consciously and unconsciously create speeded-up work rhythms. We have a vested interest in adapting to these work rhythms while at work. This is troublesome enough. Even more serious problems arise when we cannot relinquish our speeded-up existence once the workday is over.

The problem with speed and work is that we never take the time to critique the cumulative negative impact of hurry in the workplace. What do we end up doing to persons and institutions when we create work environments in which multitasking (doing multiple things at once) is a given and all tasks are always expected to be completed as soon as possible?

Hurry on the job is not just manufactured from organizational policies and practices. Powerful internal hurry factors also come into play surrounding our work. We rush to keep up with everyone else so as not to be perceived as slackers. We want to be regarded as team players. Another even more dangerous factor has to do with our overlinking what we do to who we are. If self-worth is lodged almost exclusively in the work we do and we understand speed to be integral to what we do, then speed becomes crucial to our self-identity. Speed becomes a defining element in our self-understanding. It is difficult to envision ourselves well without it. This pervasive deep dependency is one reason why so many people who feel that they need to slow down cannot.

We run to remain in control. What a paradox! The very thing that makes us feel like we are out of control may be one of the ways we try to maintain control of ourselves and our life situations. In some respects, we accommodate to the increasing speed of life because increasing speed is the only way we can imagine keeping up with the fast pace of life. It is like walking on a treadmill. As the speed is increased, we must increase our stride to a fast walk, a jog, and then a sprint. By not adjusting to the pace of the machine, we risk falling off and injuring ourselves. As long as we can keep up with the speed of the machine we maintain some semblance of control over it. Similarly, a faster living pace is seen as a necessary controlling response to the living treadmill.

We run for success. "Both Campaigning Full-Tilt to the End." "Fresh Attack Ads Fuel a Furious Finale." These are two headlines from Massachusetts papers published just before a 2002 gubernatorial election. Notice the descriptive terms *full-tilt* and *furious*. Both candidates were convinced that pushing harder and faster up to the final moment was the way to success. (We do expect political candidates to *run* for office.) Drivenness is synonymous with success in political campaigns and in many other areas of life. What are the benefits and liabilities of such a widespread, unquestioned correlation? Are we able to envision success apart from fast-paced engagement?

We run to please people. Running can be a way of endearing ourselves to people, especially when we think that by not running we somehow run the risk of letting people down. For some, one of the worst pains in life is being thought of badly by another person. It does not matter that that the judgment may be groundless and erroneous. The reality of being the object of someone's disdain is too much for some persons to bear. So they do whatever they must to avoid putting themselves in that position, including never saying no to requests and functioning as quickly as possible to make sure that complaints never arise. This self-imposed tyranny is not an isolated condition.

In *People Pleasers: Helping Others Without Hurting Yourself,* Les Carter identifies the following seven identifiers of people pleasers:

> Duty as a driving motivator
> Legitimate needs quickly set aside

Equating decisiveness with hurting others
Difficulty living within limits
Sensitivity to judgments
The need to keep life controlled
Dishonesty about who you really are

We run for the rush. We like the gushing of adrenaline in our being, the physiological boosters that have us feeling supercharged. I once sat in the airport with a friend who worked throughout our waiting together for my flight. He made several quick calls on his portable phone and seemed to be having conversations with himself when he wasn't talking on the phone or to me. Indeed, he seemed to be carrying on multiple conversations at the same time— and enjoying every minute of it. Many of us do enjoy the rush. We like the surge of energy coursing rapidly, and seemingly endlessly, through our veins. We enjoy the feeling of power that comes with being able to perform multiple tasks rapidly and efficiently. We delight in the impression of accelerated competency that we give others around us. We revel in the social and economic gains that we believe are a direct result of not just our talent but also the dexterity and swiftness of our talent.

Robert Gleik observes in *Faster: The Acceleration of Just About Everything:* "We humans have chosen speed and we thrive on it—more than we generally admit. Our ability to work fast and play fast gives us power. It thrills us. If we have learned the name of just one hormone, it is adrenaline. No wonder we call sudden exhilaration *a rush.*"[2]

We run to be first. Martin Luther King Jr. used to preach about "the drum major instinct," the common human need to be first, to lead the parade. King said that this instinct could serve us well in terms of fueling commendable ambition inside us, or it could lead to our demise. The drum major instinct could lead to an unhealthy drive to social superiority. As I reflect on it, the desire to be first may be behind some of the hurry sickness in our world. Remember what happens when a new checkout line opens up in a store: people mindlessly hurry to be served first in the new line. We all have observed persons leaving performances and games a few moments early to be the first ones out, to beat the traffic. As children, my brothers and I often yelled "firsts." "First to take a bath." "First to sit in the front seat." First to use the toaster." We wanted to secure first rights so as to not have to wait on others. As we grow, our desire to be first is rarely questioned in what is often a first-come, first-served world. Here are some questions worth pondering: Why do we find waiting so hard? Why do we need to be first in line all the time? What does our first fixation gain for us? What do we lose?

We run to get our share. This holds true at family gatherings where certain dishes are well known and move off the table with jetlike speed. The fear of being left out is the reason behind some of our dashing. Think store sales, garage sales, job fairs, and the vast assortment of special limited offers. While getting while the getting is good is an important social skill in spots, the problem arises when the fear of not getting our share runs roughshod over other values, when fear of being left out becomes the regulating thermostat for our behavior. When this happens we are relegated to living life stuck in running mode.

We run because we do not know how to stop. In the middle of a workshop on hurry and overload, a participant made this confession: "I agree with everything everyone is saying about hurry. I know that I am hurting myself. I feel the pain. I feel something else. I feel like I don't know how to stop. I feel like I do not know how to stop." We do reach a point where destructive behavior seems to exercise an unquestioned power over us, so much so that we feel powerless in its grasp. This is the bind of the deep addiction. Even when one is wrapped up tightly, a little squirming here and there will create wiggle room and will loosen the bonds. People who don't know how to stop running can begin the journey toward freedom with one small behavioral change. *Freedom is gained through being faithful to small steps.*

Notes

1. Lewis Porter, *John Coltrane: His Life and Music* (Ann Arbor: The University of Michigan Press, 1998), 36.
2. Robert Gleik, *Faster: The Acceleration of Just About Everything* (New York: Pantheon Books, 1999), 12.

Questions and Exercises

1. What do you perceive as benefits from living in a hurry? Test your perceptions. Are these true benefits? Are these benefits really worth it? What are the hidden liabilities of the benefits?

2. What do you perceive as liabilities from living in a hurry? Test your perceptions. Are the liabilities small prices to pay? Can you admit that chronic hurry is a serious threat to your quality of life?

3. Be on the lookout for "big small choices." An overloaded, overdriven life is the cumulative total of small choices we make. For example, one Saturday morning, my writing extended past the time limit I had placed on it, pushing back planned exercise. After exercise stood a lunch date with my wife and some friends. For a moment my best responsible choice seemed to be to squeeze in the exercise, then quickly shower and dress and make it to lunch. I felt uneasy

about the speed I was placing on myself. I made a big small choice: I decided not to exercise until later in the day and take my time to prepare for my lunch date. I believe the key to developing an unrushed lifestyle is focusing and making smarter choices regarding small decisions. *Success begins and ends with faithfulness to small tasks.*

4. Dropping. This is one word that can make all the difference in the world. One of the great inducements of rushing is trying to do too much. The problem with trying to do too much is that we are usually unaware of our plight. Even if you are presently unconvinced of your overload, try this for a week or so. Look at your current schedule and delete some items. Postpone or cancel some engagements. Make a list of your list of "droppings." At the end of the designated period, notice your attitude and demeanor. How do you feel? Begin to imagine a more comfortable living load as the living norm of your life.

3

running away from
aches and fears

"The reason that most of us fill up our time and stay busy is that we are afraid to be alone. We do not want to deal with everything we find in ourselves. One thing I have learned from practically fifty years of listening to people is that nearly all of us have our own inner monsters. It seems that if we will just keep busy enough, we won't have to deal with them."
— Morton Kelsey, *The Other Side of Silence*

EACH MORNING I OBSERVE MOMENTS OF SILENCE AND reflection. There are four elements to my morning experience: being still, receiving God's love, embracing personhood and community, and welcoming the day. This is my morning BREW. I support my BREW with inspirational readings and journaling. Not long after I started beginning my day in this way, I noticed something: uninvited things began to surface inside of me. As I observed my holy margin time in the morning, things that were submerged under the waters of conscious awareness floated to the top. This would have been fine except for the fact that some of the things that floated up were uncomfortable fears and distressing pains. At first when I noticed this happening, I moved quickly to press the button of positive thinking in my head, to push these uncomfortable thoughts back under water. Gradually I realized that allowing my hidden pains to surface was healthy and healing. I noticed that noticing my hurts and not denying them made me feel stronger.

Running from things that threaten us is instinctive. I remember having nightmares as a youngster that caused me to yell out in terror, and occasionally run down the hallway of our house. I remember my father catching me one night and shaking me back to safe reality. Fear made me run.

Though running from threatening circumstances may be instinctive, it is also learned behavior for most of us. We are responsibly and wisely taught to flee persons or situations we perceive as dangerous. Thus, earlier on in our lives we are made to run through instinct and instruction.

Taking flight is not the problem; taking flight as a way of life is the problem. Running can be a means of liberating escape or oppressive avoidance. I wonder if our hurried living is more about keeping things down than it is about getting things done. How much of our fast motion has to do with an unconscious need to remain unfocused on distressing reality? We are afraid that if we stop, the painful truth of our deepest angst will break us. This is the plight of Violet in Toni Morrison's stirring novel, *Jazz:*

> They fill their minds and hands with soap and repair
> and dicey confrontations because what is waiting
> for them, in a suddenly idle moment, is the seep of
> rage. Molten. Thick and slow-moving. Mindful and

particular about what in its path it chooses to bury.

Or else, into a beat of time, and sideways under their breasts, slips a sorrow they don't know where from.[1]

There is greater danger in suppressing our pain and fears through running away from them than in stopping long enough to examine them.

First, dodged distress festers. I usually light a candle and set it in front of me before I write. This flickering flame is a source of writing inspiration. But this small support can possibly lead to great heartache if I forget to blow it out. Initially the fire would be small and insignificant, but it would not remain this way. Each small flame has the potential to end up as a great fire. By not attending to our fears we fan their flame inside of us.

Second, by not attending to the troubles inside we miss the chance to grasp the teaching and transformative power inside of them. I want to be careful not to minimize the pain of heartache. Heartache is hard. If there were signs that read, "Trouble Up Ahead," most of us would head in another direction. But some of you reading this would continue toward the trouble in spite of the sign. You would keep traveling not because you are masochistic but because you know that pain is ultimately unavoidable. And you know something else: hurt can become an avenue for positive transformation. In some instances, the pain will not go away, will not leave, precisely because it is trying to tell us something, to show us something.

One of the great examples of the transformative power of pain is Jesus' experience in the Garden of Gethsemane. I do not believe Gethsemane was a hoax or a put-on. The depth of Jesus' anguish about his impending demise that ominous night was as thick as his relentless compassion for others. Yet Jesus did not diminish his pain by running head-long into last-minute ministry matters. He did not try to fit in as much as he could as fast as he could. He slowed to a crawl, and then to a complete stop, and attended complete-ly to his inner turmoil, as recorded in Mark 14:33-38:

> He took with him Peter and James and John, and began to be distressed and agitated. And said to them, "I am deeply grieved, even to death; remain here, and keep awake." And going a little farther, he threw himself on the ground and prayed that, if it were possible, the hour might pass from him. He said, "Abba, Father, for you all things are possible; remove this cup from me; yet, not what I want, but what you want." He came and found them sleeping; and he said to Peter, "Simon, are you asleep? Could you not keep awake one hour? Keep awake and pray that you may not come into the time of trial; the spirit indeed is willing, but the flesh is weak."

Jesus encountered pain in his fear of the future, his sense of being abandoned by his weary disciples, and his fear that his most trusted disciple would not be able to stand the test that awaited him.

Jesus could have chosen to deny his troubles inside. Instead he gave full attention to them. He leaned into the ten-sion mounting up inside of him. In this way, in holding his fears before him, Jesus defused his fears. Jesus gained power over disempowerment and ultimately access to a new and glorious resurrected life. Unlike Jesus, we tend to be afraid of our fears. We deny them, sometimes in the name of Jesus, as opposed to confronting them in the manner of Jesus.

According to Henri Nouwen, fear keeps us from execut-ing one of life's most effective anti-hurry actions: waiting.

In our particular historical situation, waiting is even more difficult because we are so fearful. One of the most pervasive emotions in the atmosphere around us is fear. People are afraid—afraid of inner feelings, afraid of other people, and also afraid of the future. Fearful people have a hard time waiting, because when we are afraid we want to get away from where we are. Our fears keep us running; our running keeps us afraid.[2]

Hurry is not the only way to run way from our fears. We have many forms of escape. One unspoken but prevalent method is by choosing to remain confused about something: selective ignorance. Confusion frees us from responsibility. I once heard someone say that the hardest thing to do in life is to awaken someone who is pretending to be asleep. We nurture confusion inside of ourselves by purposely resisting deepening awareness and clarity.

One example of sustained confusion is continued institutional impotency on matters of justice and equity in the face of convincing analyses and solutions. As I have sat on committees charged with eradicating racism and sexism in educational organizations and town government, I have observed what I call feigned ignorance used as a strategy for continuing obvious oppression. This happens when an institution chooses to remain in the dark about how it practices oppression through its structures and foundations. Institutional structures and foundations refer to how an organization functions and its underlying purposes and historic traditions for functioning. When injustice is found within attitudes and actions of personnel, policies, and overt practices, change is not overwhelmingly difficult. Change is more elusive when an organization confronts its basic structures and foundations. This is the point at which usually assertively keen minds begin to conveniently slumber. Blindness is perceived as being more beneficial than sight. This is a choice to maintain organizational oppression through persistent nonseeing.

Persons choose to remain in the dark outside the workplace as well. Have you ever suspected something bad about a loved one but resisted knowing the truth so as to not have your worst fears realized? This is a way of running from pain through selective ignorance in our personal lives. There are some things we would rather not know. We fear that the truth will be too much to handle.

Let's continue focusing on ways we run from our fears for a moment. Avoiding tension and conflict is another way we run. In a world filled with violence, it is understandable why we would want to be where conflict situations are not. This is an even more pressing desire for persons reared in violent homes or regularly victimized by domestic violence or employee abuse. Yet conflict is a reality of life. Running away from tension will not change that. On the contrary, a pattern of running away from conflict adds to violence. Running from conflict ensures that the conditions that make for conflict will remain. Running from tension is a way of conspiring with tension-causing agents. While some conflict should and must be avoided (e.g., life-threatening situations), some conflict must be faced and engaged. In these cases, not touching tension and confronting conflict is a serious affront to life.

In his legendary *Letter from a Birmingham Jail*, Martin Luther King Jr. answered the charge from church leaders that by leading sit-ins, marches, and other forms of direct action he was irresponsibly creating dangerous chaos in Birmingham. King responded by daringly and creatively challenging the notion that tension is always bad. He explained that the goal of direct action is to create tension and, in turn, generate new resolve to work for justice. Knowing that his advocacy of such tension would sound strange to clergy trained to smooth over rough places, King broke new theological ground (ground that still awaits scholarly nurturing). He suggested that tension is more than a social-change strategy. It is an important life principle: "My citing the creation of tension as part of the work of the nonviolent resister may sound rather shocking. But I must confess that I am not afraid of the word 'tension.' I have earnestly opposed violent tension, but there is a type of constructive, nonviolent tension which is necessary for growth."[3]

We can also run from our fears by shrinking our weaknesses and inflating our strengths. In the fall of 2002, I saw a television advertisement for a new toy called Shrinky Dinks. The toy is a small machine that allows you to shrink paper products such as pictures and stickers. One way of not owning up to a fear or pain is by lessening its weight of importance in our minds. We discount the problem by convincing ourselves that it is not a problem. We do this easily with our hurts. Hurt minimization is behind the admonition we hear early on, "Big kids don't cry." Weakness deflation is usually combined with strength inflation. Often persons maintain their addictions through the illusion of ableness: "This may have done someone else in, but I am in control. I know what I am doing. Don't worry about me; I'll be just fine." Inflating strengths is akin to putting on a costume. Costumed strength is pseudo-strength, false strength.

Finally, we run from our fears by avoiding suffering. Who in their right mind wants to suffer? Who wants to endure pain and heartache, especially when avenues of exit are clearly marked and readily accessible? Running away from sure suffering is only human.

But surety of suffering is a part of the human condition. This means that our suspicion of those who live to suffer may be matched by a curiosity about those who learn through their suffering. I do not say what I am about to say as someone who is fully at ease with the redemptive reality of suffering. Nothing could be further from the truth. I say it because ordinary persons have provided us with extraordinary witness of its truth: Certain suffering teaches certain things we are unable to learn otherwise. Nouwen remembers such a witness:

> I was invited to visit a friend who was very sick. He was a man about fifty-three years old who had lived a very active, useful, faithful, creative life. Actually, he was a social activist who had cared deeply for people. When he was fifty he found out he had cancer, and the cancer became more and more severe.
>
> When I came to him, he said to me, "Henri, here I am lying in this bed, and I don't even know how to think about being sick. My whole way of thinking about myself is in terms of action, in terms of doing things for people. My life is valuable because I've been able to do many things for many people. And suddenly, here I am, passive, and I can't do anything anymore." And he said to me, "Help me to think about this situation in a new way. Help me to think about not being able to do anything anymore so I won't be driven to despair. Help me to understand what it means that now all sorts of people are doing things to me over which I have no control."[4]

Nouwen's friend was leaning into a new learning about human existence. His suffering was forcing him to define life in terms other than power and control, to live life with muted power and control. By overfixating on power and control, we defile life. Overliving through power and control is a way of snuffing out Spirit, divine and human. Only through balancing power with vulnerability and control with faith can we live empowered and free.

Notes

1. Toni Morrison, *Jazz* (New York: Penguin Books, 1992), 16.
2. Henri Nouwen, "A Spirituality of Waiting," in *Living with God in the World,* ed. John S. Mogabgab (Nashville: Upper Room Books, 1993), 65–66.
3. Martin Luther King Jr., "Letter from a Birmingham Jail" in *A Testimony of Hope: The Essential Writings of Martin Luther King, Jr.,* ed. James Melvin Washington (San Francisco: Harper & Row, 1986), 291.
4. Henri Nouwen, "A Spirituality of Waiting," 70–71.

Exercises

1. Reread Morton Kelsey's quote at the beginning of this chapter. Begin to imagine a monster. It would be better for you to draw your monster on a piece of paper or in your journal. Think of and draw three or four monsters. When you are done sit still and silent for five or so minutes. When you are ready, name your monsters. Once you have identified your great fears, have a written or thoughtful dialogue with them over the next days and weeks. Ask questions and listen. Go to the root of your fear.

2. You may undertake the foregoing procedure with other deep realities in your life. Try imaging and reflecting on your sorrows and regrets.

4

running away from ourselves

"But when he came to himself ... "
—Luke 15:17

"Up and down the block, house lights come on, and children shoo cats out of front doors. The hills over the town flatten, grow larger with the dark. There's no help for it, but Pinky feels a melancholy he's hard put to explain, and it has to do with the onset of dark and the sudden still....

"And he sees it has to do with fear—the way we run through our lives in terror of it."
—Claire Davis,
"Labors of the Heart"

"When I see a baby quietly staring at his or her own hands ... or a toddler off in a corner putting something into a cup and then taking it out, over and over again ... or a preschooler lying in the grass daydreaming, I like to think that they, in their own ways, are 'alone in

*the best room' of their houses, using the solitude they
need to find the courage to grow."*
—Fred Rogers, *You Are Special:
Words of Wisdom from America's
Most Beloved Neighbor*

THE FOLLOWING WAS REPORTED TO ME AS BEING A true story, though the name may be different. A man ran into a meeting asking for Joel. Those gathered in the room looked at each other in utter astonishment. Then they all began to laugh, thinking that it was a joke. How could it be otherwise, since the man asking for Joel was Joel? Laughter turned to concern when Joel, replaying his gaffe and hearing it for the first time, exited the room embarrassed and dismayed. As amazing as this mistake is, can you say that it did not occur, beyond a shadow of doubt?

Our doubt is fed by ominous reality. Although few of us have served as a magician's subject in a disappearing act, many of us know what it is like to feel vanished. We have ways of expressing this: "I don't know whether I am coming or going." "I don't know who I am anymore." "I feel like my life is passing me by." "Get a life." "If my head wasn't attached to my body, I'd lose it." "I feel like I am losing it." "I'm not feeling like myself." "She is not herself." Can you think of similar expressions of human vanishing? How can we allow ourselves to simply disappear?

Joel's saving grace was his sense of his own missing and his being in search of himself. His public inquiry was indicative of a private yearning. Too many of us do not know that we are missing, or worse, have accepted our absence from ourselves.

Self-numbing

I have a new dentist who happens to work swiftly. The second time I went to him I thought he was moving too fast; he had forgotten something. He explained the procedure to me, we laughed when I asked if there would be a pop quiz on the subject, and then he and his assistant went to work. They were about a minute into the preliminary drilling when a disturbing thought popped into my head: I had not been administered any numbing medication. Though I wasn't feeling any pain at the time, I knew that in a few moments, I would be ready to die. With the certainty of suffering on the horizon, I mumbled, "You haven't given me anything for the pain." My dentist stopped and calmly asked, "Do you feel anything?" When I confirmed his informed suspicion that I didn't, he said in a matter-of-fact sort of way, "That's because there is no nerve in the tooth I'm working on. You have a root canal there. No nerve, no feeling." "Oh," I said, "carry on." But being numb to life is not nearly as desirable as what I felt or didn't feel during my dental visit.

Hurry makes us numb to life. To be numb is not to feel anything, to be free of the feeling of life. Not to feel life is not to experience life. Have you ever gone through a day and wondered where it went? The problem was not the day's going but our going and going to the point of not noticing anything throughout the day. Hurry is a desensitizer, snuffing out moments of intimacy with life to the point that we get used to living day after day with little deep feeling or passion.

Self-numbness is not feeling the you that you are. It is facilitated by our being crowded by overload and drivenness. Have you heard those radio commercials in which the speaker begins to speak very fast at the end in order to fit in legally required but marketing-irrelevant text? The words become garbled and the message indistinguishable. How many persons listen to this harried talk? How many persons can? I think the common response is turning off our attention to the commercial once it reaches the word-racing stage. We stop listening; we numb ourselves to the message.

Hurry makes us numb; it saps the feeling of authentic aliveness. By authentic aliveness, I mean life in a rudimentary spiritual sense, unadorned by accessories, even laudable ones such as enjoyable work. The great sage Abraham Heschel once said, "Just to be is a blessing; just to live is holy." Before there is living to do, to acquire, and to satisfy there is first living, life itself.

Two thousand years ago, Jesus said, "The kingdom of God is among [within] you" (Luke 17:21). This is a striking observation, especially when you consider that conditions and prerequisites are not given. There is always something amazingly wonderful inside of us that we have nothing to do with being there. It is a gift. Before there are the privileges of life, there is the privilege of life itself. This is the place of utter defilement where hurry is concerned: being numb to knowing that *merely being is a blessing and just living is holy.*

The hideous chain reaction of being numb to ourselves is being numb to others and all of creation. Anthony DeMello defines this condition as sleepwalking: "Most people, even though they don't know it, are asleep. They're born asleep, they live asleep, they die in their sleep without ever waking up. They never understand the loveliness and the beauty of this thing that we call human existence."[1] How often do you sense yourself missing yourself? What are you going to do about it?

Self-noticing

Constant rushing serves to keep us numb to ourselves as precious children of God. We become too busy to notice the depth of our riches, to notice who we are and what we have in having life. The answer to self-numbing is self-noticing. Self-noticing is a sacred calling.

Self-noticing is the hidden message of the gospel, the message that goes unheard due to our fixation on the gospel's call for self-denial. But think about it a moment. What is the essential prerequisite for practicing self-denial?—sufficiently experiencing self to begin with. Without the experience of authentic selfhood, self-denial is a hoax, a sham. The gospel is as much a call for self-is-ness as it is a critique of selfishness.

Throughout his brief but dynamic ministry, Jesus was constantly rescuing people from the deathly tides of self-diminishment. He was especially concerned about women, children, the sick, and the victims of cultural racism, such as that despised lot known as Samaritans. These groups of persons were the least, the last, and the lost, according to social, political, and religious beliefs. They lived under the iron boot of social and personal oppression. Constantly bearing the brunt of sustained overt and covert social assault, many of them internalized the dehumanizing social definitions assigned to them. By believing lies about who they were or not questioning them, they unwittingly conspired with their diminishment.

Jesus danced on the waters of human diminishment in holy defiance. With effortless humility and expansive grace, he loved the unlovable and touched the untouchable. His message was unquestionably self-affirming. How could it be otherwise, given that his ultimate mission was to impress upon us all how much we are loved by God? To fully receive love is to know that one is worth being loved. Who are we to barely notice or completely miss what God beholds always, with limitless compassion and esteem? Good theology honors divinity and humanity in the same breath. Good worship praises God freely without diminishing God's people in the least.

There are many marvelous pictures in *Seeing Jazz: Artists and Writers on Jazz*. One of my favorites was taken in 1941 by Milt Hinton. Hinton captured Cozy Cole, Danny Barker, and Chad Collins in a posture of greeting each other. In this perfectly proportioned, black-and-white picture (taken in my native New Orleans), the three men are tipping their hats and bowing to each other. It is a mundane, magical moment in which three African American men in the pre-Civil Rights Movement deep South are offering to each other what a society poisoned by segregation denied them: respect. Just one look at the photograph and it is obvious that the subjects are doing more than merely welcoming each other; they are honoring each other.

We can be so busy running here, there, and everywhere that we fail to notice, welcome, and honor the gift of personhood. Permit me this gentle scolding: how dare we? This frequent but unacceptable not noticing is a way of disrespecting ourselves and our Creator. What would happen if we saw ourselves and others as God sees each of us?—a revolution in intrapersonal and interpersonal relationships the likes of which this world suffers to see.

Cherishing Your Essence

While walking one morning, I listened to one of my favorite singers, the late Eva Cassidy. One song grabbed me and would not let me go. I kept pressing the replay button over and over again, for at least a mile. Now you can be awed by Eva Cassidy's voice alone. This stunning voice applied to Stevie Wonder's thoughtful lyrics is a wonder of its own. The song *I Can Only Be Me* celebrates the gift of personal uniqueness in hallowed, heart-moving ways. His words remind us that "You can only be you, As I can only be me."

We all have an essential, core me-ness. Perhaps this is what Søren Kierkegaard had in mind when he suggested that one "be that self which one truly is." It may be covered and scarred, but it is always there. It is God's unique fingerprint on you. It is your essence, without which you would not be the unique person you are. It is this essence that we must see and salute in ourselves and others. It is that part of us that we must own as is because it is who we are. This is the me that you can and should only be. It is not a sad predicament. Never before in all of history has there been a you, nor will there be ever again. This is a glorious fact of time and eternity, too astounding to go unnoticed. Moreover, we must begin to see it as a sacred calling, in the words of Kierkegaard, "to be that self which one truly is."

Cheering Your Emergence

There is a part of us already whole and beloved as is, and there is a part of us that is ever evolving. We are evolving selves. Something about us is fantastically fixed; something about is creatively changing. This is our growing self, our transforming self, the self that needs to traverse the terrain of unfamiliar places in order to live. This is the self the writer M. C. Richards refers to as "the changing, changeful person."

If our essence needs revering, our expansion needs cheering. We have entered a danger zone. We are afraid not just of the unfamiliar but also the loss of the familiar. Most of us are frightened by the prospect and experience of change. Perhaps our fears would be lessened if we took more time to sit with them and then coax them to join us in cheering on the emerging self. The best change is not for change's sake but for transformation's sake, for the sake of experiencing life afresh. Did not Jesus come that we might have more abundant life?

Slowing down helps us to notice the pulsations of new life inside of us. To this end, I believe that sometimes we need to take well days off. These are days in which we are not sick but rather deliberately supportive of our wellness, especially our deepest dreams and aspirations. On well days you can ponder where you are and where it is you feel you want to go. These are days to grieve missed opportunities, and even more, urge on surging aspirations. These are days to water new imaginings and to tend to fresh hopes. On well days, you receive (not make or take) time to cheer your emerging self onward.

When we do not observe time to cheer on our emerging selves, we quickly succumb to fear and doubt. We become easy prey to negative thinking that takes the wind out of new ideas before they have a chance to soar. There is a gnawing barrenness inside, an emptiness we cannot explain. Everyday life becomes a dirty shade of gray. We become manufacturers of our own misery. We become people of the rut.

We need time to wait with our fears and wait for confidence to rise inside of us. With confidence welling up inside, we can break through fear to positive transformation. We can dance toward our boldest dreams.

An Unexpected Accomplice

The great presumption of some religious teachings, including some understandings in Christianity, is that spiritual ascent depends on self-depreciation. This is fed in part by our disdain for selfishness and narcissism. Yet it is possible to go too far to the other extreme, to overdiminish and underappreciate the self to an extent that God frowns upon.

The consequences can be insidious and dire. For example, many religious persons remain in conditions of abuse because they have been taught loads about the value of self-denial and suffering and nothing at all about their glory. The very impulse to reject abusive behavior is stunted by a fundamental muting of human confidence. When the diminishment is religiously based, mere questioning is difficult. Oppression becomes concretized.

Good religion breaks the rock of human crushing. Good religion affirms God and God's creation in the same breath. It is my belief that God would have it no other way. Selfishness may be sinful. Self-is-ness is not. Self-is-ness is noticing, even daring to cherish and cheer who you are. To believe this is to approach not narcissism but necessary gratitude. One loves, creates, and grows more freely in the waters of self-acceptance. Sacred self-acceptance nurtures a great grace: a genius for accepting others. When we run away from ourselves, we run away from it all.

Note

1. Anthony DeMello, *Awareness: A DeMello Spirituality Conference in His Own Words* (New York: Doubleday, 1990), 5.

Exercise: Create a Well Day

This chapter has been about noticing yourself sufficiently enough that you resist conspiring with your diminishment and you use your power to imagine, create, and live life at a healthier and holier pace. This is a lifelong process, and one that involves developing new disciplines. One such discipline is what I call a well day. Set aside a day to focus on your wellness. Plan it in advance, and plan some of the day's activities, leaving sufficient margin for surprise and spontaneity. Be sure to include time for doing the things that bring you joy and space for solitude.

5

running away from God

"As I read the Old and New Testaments I am
struck by the awareness therein of our lives being
connected with cosmic powers, angels, and archangels,
heavenly principalities and powers and the groaning
of creation. It's too radical, too uncontrolled for many
of us, so we build churches which are the safest
possible places in which to escape God."
—Madeleine L'Engle, Glimpses of Grace

"We confess that we are afraid of You."
—James Melvin Washington,
Conversations with God

I WILL NEVER FORGET A VERY SPECIAL CLASS SES-
SION at Andover Newton Theological School in fall
2002. My colleague, Professor Sharon Thornton, and I
were co-teaching a course that sought to better inte-
grate the roles of prophet and pastor in the minds and

hearts of our students. In this particular class session, as usual we sat in our regular fifteen-person circle. Professor Thornton, leader for the day, explained to us all that she was not going to talk about the main points of her newly published book, *Broken Yet Beloved,* but rather about the experiences and influences behind the writing of the book. She expressed some concern about voicing things she had never talked about before. Nonetheless, she began talking at first about her childhood and the hospitable spirit of her immigrant mother. Slowly, with humor and tender emotion, she introduced us to other persons and events that helped nurture her conviction that a welcoming acceptance of all, including the least, the last, and the lost, is crucial to pastoral ministry. At points during her presentation, I would jot down a note or two to remind myself of a question I wanted to raise later. Most of the students were not writing. Their eyes were fixed on Professor Thornton. I was struck by the intensity of their focus. When she was done, we all clapped out of gratitude. I remember turning to her and saying, "Thank you for letting us see what makes you, you."

Thank God for casual relationships. Every meeting matters. With most people, we do not desire to go beyond surface familiarity and casual conversation. But we have the precious option to choose to experience deeper relationships with persons. We have the chance to get to know people, and getting to know someone better is one of life's unheralded blessings. The blessing is not without responsibility. To really get to know someone, we must be willing to focus attention on them, to listen and receive. Our knowing better is not just a matter of what they are willing to share but what we are willing to receive.

Intimacy with God works the same way. How do we ever expect to know God more deeply if we are too busy to stop, notice, listen, and receive?

Being Still and Knowing God

Knowing God requires only that we live. No one alive is ever out of range of God's presence and blessing. Knowing God more deeply, however, requires our willingness to stop, notice, listen, and receive. While you may be in range of God, inattentiveness may render you powerless to pick up God's sacred signals.

That we can know God is perhaps the most astounding assertion of biblical truth. God is directly knowable not just in sacred ritual and encounters or epiphanies but also, wonder of wonders, in everyday life experience. In Exodus, the everydayness of God's presence is realized through eating bread or manna from heaven in the grit and grime of desert journeying. God is apart of the natural ebb and flow of everyday life for biblical Israel. But the everydayness of God does not automatically result in increased knowledge about God and deeper friendship with God. Knowledge of God and friendship with God depend not just on God's offering but also on our receptivity. Significantly, Hebrew theology teaches that deepening faith cannot occur apart from the purposeful choice to be still. Jesus' frequent practice of stillness and solitude shows he fully accepted such practices as a way to know God more deeply. Stillness was integral to Jesus' deepening relationship with and commitment to the one he comfortably referred to as "Father."

Hurry: an Enemy of Stillness

If stillness is such a crucial aspect of spiritual intimacy and growth, how can we allow ourselves to live with so little of it? Moreover, the unquestioned prioritization in holy Scripture unmasks chronic hurry for what it is: an enemy of stillness, and consequentially an enemy of deeper friendship with God. Hurry is a serious threat to the deepening spiritual life available to us all in all walks of life, not just called religious people. The gifts of stillness cannot be realized with our present fixation on hurry. We cannot give ourselves permission to be still as long as we are addicted to hurry. Hurry is a spiritual issue.

As we slow ourselves, we become better able to perceive and receive the blessings of stillness for deepening our relationship to God. Stillness helps us to engage two important movements where God is concerned: discerning God and receiving God.

Discerning God

Rushing severely hampers our ability to discern the ineffable mystery of God in the mysterious and ordinary blessings of ordinary life, those things that are beyond us and those things that are right in front of us. One of the best ways to apprehend God's reality is to show up in life. This is portable devotion, worship that is not limited to precise times and special places. It is possible at any time; discernment determines whether or not we are awake within such moments.

Alice Walker reminds us in her astonishing novel that God is in the field with "the color purple." But divinity does not just loiter around the strikingly beautiful. One of the most memorable classroom moments I have ever had involved our thinking about God as experienced in the grime and grit of life. One student spoke of how she discerned God in a setting that reeked with the scent of human waste. Another relayed as a sacred discerning of God growing up on a farm and receiving the fond embrace of his father who was dirtied from head to toe from having worked in the dirt all day long. Another student came up to me in tears after class. She briefly shared with me in person what she could not find the strength to share in class, that she had discerned God in the face of a Junkie. This impromptu class session gave rise to our reverent imaging of divinity as "dirty God": the God who is present in the muck and the mire as well as the miraculous. That indeed is one of the greatest miracles of all.

Our hurried existence keeps us from discerning God, including discerning new dimensions of God. This is risky running, especially when, in the words of the climactic song from the movie *The Color Purple,* "Maybe God is trying to tell [us] something."

Receiving God

Let me go back to the experience in the classroom with the professor who shared her personal odyssey. Remember, I told you that instead of taking notes, students were fixed on the professor. They hung on her every word and gesture. We were engaging knowledge in an alternative way, less by hard reflection and more by soft reception. Critical reflection is a crucial, I would argue even sacred, way of engaging knowledge. However, human reasoning is not the only way to know. We know as well by sensing, feeling, intuiting, and being open. We know through means that are suprarational, means that go beyond thinking. These alternative ways of knowing are no less valuable to us than is hard-nosed reasoned reflection. Indeed, relying solely on reason for our knowing severely restricts the scope of our knowledge. There is much reality beyond the reach of human reasoning. This is nowhere truer than in matters related to spirit, our ideas of ultimate truth, and the ineffable reality of God. God is too big for human comprehension. We must traverse alternative avenues to divinity to more fully engage the Divine.

This is why silence is so important. Silence is a way of slowing and stopping ourselves and our thoughts. This creates space to experience God in new and deeply liberating ways. Silence helps us to experience God beyond our parochial, prejudiced, self-serving ideas of God. Silence opens the windows of our hearts to allow the fresh breeze of God's limitless reality to blow through. Silence forces us to let God be God on God's terms, not ours. Silence reminds us that God is always much more than our potentially helpful or hurtful perceptions and rationalizations. Silence challenges reason's monopoly on God by ushering other ways (feeling, sensing, experiencing) of knowing God to the table.

Do you see why chronic hurry and deepening spirituality are essentially incompatible? We need time and silence to know God more fully. Inasmuch as hurry frustrates silence, it is an enemy to a deepening awareness of the loving Mystery, of God in Christ Jesus, of the Holy Spirit, of the unutterable reality of God.

When was the last time that you heard God whisper, "I love you"?

Denise Levertov captures our flight away from divinity in her prayer/poem "Flickering Mind."

Mind:

Lord, not you,
it is I who am absent.
At first
belief was a joy I kept in secret,
stealing alone
into sacred places:
a quick glance, and away—and back,
circling.
I have long since uttered your name
but now
I elude your presence.
I stop to think about you, and my mind
at once
like a minnow darts away,
darts
into the shadows, into gleams that fret
unceasing over
the river's purling and passing.
Not for one second
will my self hold still, but wanders
anywhere,
everywhere it can turn. Not you,
it is I who am absent.
You are the stream, the fish, the light,
the pulsing shadow,
you are the unchanging presence, in whom all
moves and changes.

How can I focus my flickering, perceive
at the fountain's heart
the sapphire I know is there?[1]

Note

1. Denise Levertov, "Flickering Mind," from *A Door in the Hive,*
   copyright © 1989 by Denise Levertov. Reprinted by permission of New Directions Publishing Corporation, New York,
   New York.

Exercise and Reflection:
Where Do You Experience God?

Write inside the circles and ovals realities where you experience God, a sense of the sacred, or a feeling of enhanced meaning. Examples include your beliefs about God, movement, stillness, silence, and conversation.

Take a moment to reflect on your God spots. How many areas were you able to name? What sorts of things did you identify? Is there any one area where you experience God the most? What did you put in the largest/smallest circles? As you ponder your list, is there anything you left out?

We experience God, holiness, and transcendence throughout life. Our experience of God is earthy, and our experience of earth is godly.

Take another look at your circles. I suspect that you have identified things from everyday life. This is as it should be, because God cannot be compartmentalized into religious days, seasons, festival, and observances. Perhaps this is why Jesus felt free to communicate great spiritual truths by referring to such everyday, mundane things as lamp stands, bushel baskets, and mustard seeds. He used the ordinary around persons to explode the extraordinary inside of persons.

I have an image of three entities on a dance floor: God, life, and humanity. When we would get too comfortably individualistic and pietistic in our religious pursuits, I envision God throwing us back into the arms of life. When we would get too much at ease with life bereft of sacred meanings and interpretations, I envision life flinging us back into the arms of God. Our experience of God is earthy, and our experience of this earth is godly.

In his theology of the incarnation, the apostle Paul offers a zenith of an example of God in life and life in God. In Philippians 2:5-8, Paul speaks of God "being born in human likeness, and being found in human form," and, even more striking, "becom[ing] obedient to the point of death—even death on a cross." How much earthier can God get than that? Since sacred reality pervades all of life, the most important continuing action of life is paying attention.

6

the savoring pace alternative

"As a deer longs for flowing streams, so my soul longs for you, O God."
—Psalm 42:1

"Come to me, all you that are weary and are carrying heavy burdens, and I will give you rest."
—Matthew 11:28

JESUS DID NOT JUST PROMISE REST. HE LIVED A MORE relaxed stride than we generally believe. If Jesus were around in the flesh today, his pace would drive us nuts. Here is a man who loitered in Jerusalem as a lad, who would not be rushed into judgment against "a woman caught in adultery," and who did not respond to every demand on him with an as-soon-as-possible response. Remember, he arrived four days late for Lazarus's funeral.

In *Rest in the Storm: Self-Care Strategies for Clergy and Other Caregivers,* I discuss Jesus' alternative sacred pace, calling it a pace characterized by peace, patience, and atten-tiveness. Granted, there are those instances in Scripture when Jesus moved "immediately" to do something. But such immediacy may be interpreted with urgency in mind, not rushing. Moreover, his immediate motions occurred within in an overall living pace that was more deliberate than speedy. If Jesus, of all people, felt he had God's permis-sion to take his time, what about us? Jesus was not the only one graced to live a more healthy, sustainable, and enjoyable pace; we all are.

You don't have to settle for being hooked on hurry, espe-cially given the enormous toll it takes on our quality of life. There are too many serious liabilities and losses involved.

I have a proposal for you: the prospect of imagining and choosing an alternative to hurry. I believe this proposal will provide you with more peace and fulfillment than hurry can ever give you. Receiving my proposal involves two motions on your part: imagining and choosing.

Two Essential Breakthroughs

You have to dare to imagine, force yourself to conjecture that there is a better way. One of the greatest biblical truths of all is "as a person thinks so is she or he." In order to beat hurry in our lives, we have to beat it in our minds. This will mean identifying those beliefs that have us running. We must see the belief switches that cause us to practice hurry and overload and move to turn these switches off, to believe differently. For example, turn off the belief switch that says you are what you do. Substitute for it the truth that your worth comes from who you are and not what you do. Turn off the belief switch that says committed living demands your exhaustion. Put in its place an understanding that you can live a life of commitment to family, vocation, and society without inflicting violence on yourself. Turn off the belief switch that says you don't deserve rest until you are ready to drop. Begin to believe that rest is a gift from God to be regularly observed in order to prevent us from ever getting to the point of breakdown.

Cultivating new understandings about such things as work, rest, and even your views on what God desires of you is the key to breaking hurry addiction. If you don't change the way you think, old thinking will ultimately sabotage any effort at change, no matter how sincere your desire to change. Change begins in your mind, by giving yourself permission to imagine new principles on which to lead and regulate your life.

Imagining an alternative living pace is the first major breakthrough in the battle against hurry. Choosing to live out what you imagine is the second major breakthrough. The inducements to hurry are manifold and potent. What we believe in our inner world and what we experience in the wider world are constantly pushing and shoving us toward a pace that is faster and faster. With all due respect to the forces that force hurry upon us, they do not have the final word; we do.

We can decide that we are not going to take it anymore. We can decide that addiction to hurry is unacceptable. I am writing this section in December 2002. Forty-seven years ago, in December 1955, a woman by the name of Rosa Parks made a decision. She decided that she was not going to stand up on a bus in Montgomery and give her seat to a passenger who had boarded after her. In that segregated society that prevailed in the not-too-distant past, courtesy was not the issue; justice was. Parks exercised her power of choice, and in doing so she galvanized a protest sentiment that helped fuel human rights movements around the world. Parks made change happen by exercising her power to choose.

In his classic, *Man's Search for Meaning*, Holocaust survivor Viktor E. Frankl calls the power to choose "the last of the human freedoms." It is the freedom, Frankl declares, "to choose one's attitude in any given set of circumstances, to choose one's own way."

The point is this: *We have the power to un-choose hurry.*

My re-imagining and un-choosing regarding hurry began in the summer of 1998.

Dreaming a New Pace

Toward the end of the summer of 1998, I felt myself grieving. It was a grief that was something more than regret that a time of more play and less labor was coming to a close. As I struggled to name what I was feeling, it dawned inside of me that what saddened me was the sense of a pending loss. What I feared losing at summer's end was a more relaxed, peaceful, and patient living pace that I had fallen into or that had fallen into me.

I noticed it during a cruise to Alaska. A financial blessing made it possible for my wife and me to take the dream vacation we had talked about since the beginning of our marriage eighteen years prior. It was the trip that tripped me up in several life-giving ways. First, I was awed by the vastness of the waterways we traveled. I had seen great bodies of water before, but for the first time in my life I was in great masses of water for days. From our large window, I marveled at all the water; it didn't seem to end, and I thought that it was as deep as it was wide. Second, the glaciers stopped me: towering masses that were not green or brown but white. Louisiana, my home state, had not afforded me such sightings. Perhaps the most astounding vision of all for me was the streams rolling down the sides of mountains. Not just seeing them but hearing them brought me to extended pauses and complete stops. While I expected that the trip to Alaska would be a memorable one, I did not expect that it would move me so.

As I thought about it more and more, I began to realize that my summer-ending grief was connected to Alaska in some way. It wasn't so much a missing of the special places but the savoring pace—the pauses and the stops—to which the places in Alaska had called me and were continuing to call me.

In calling me *to* something, Alaska was calling me *away* from something. While on the cruise and in the wake of it, I began to sense that I was living life much too fast. To be sure, this matter had been raised before in my head and heart. There had been times when I had wished that I had completed my senior year with my class instead of rushing off to college to get a head start. In addition, I had thought on occasion that earning my initial graduate degree in divinity at an accelerated clip may have had some downsides. There were also moments when I felt that productive pastorates in three churches over a fifteen-year period had sort of whizzed by. And, there were those times when I had looked at one or another of our four children and thought, "Are they growing up too fast, or am I just not seeing the stages?" Concern for my fast pace had nagged at me. In Alaska and its aftermath, the pace whisper inside of me became a full-fledged protest.

The first stage of the protest was the grief I began to feel about having to get back up to speed after having slowed or been slowed in Alaska. The grief led to anger. I began to say to myself in various ways, "I will not go back to running and rushing through life. If life were meant to be lived on the run, then slowing down would not feel so good; it would not feel so refreshing and right; I would not grieve its loss so." The anger led to resolve, a decision to live life at what I call a savoring pace: a speed that allows for thinking more deeply, listening more carefully, and seeing more clearly.

I do not remember when I first thought and said to myself, "savoring pace." I do remember that it was in response to my feeling that what was bubbling inside of me needed to be expressed fundamentally and regularly in the positive "savor more" as opposed to in the negative "slow down." The difference is important. Peace is not merely the absence of tension but is also the presence of harmony and justice. Peace is not simply a negation of something; it is the active presence of something. Likewise, savoring pace is not just the negation or the minimizing of hurry in life; it is the celebration of noticing and paying attention more in life.

We go through so much of our lives barely noticing. After a while, we accept the fact that the numbing drudgery of a life that ensues is just the way it is. Oh, there are periods, moments of deep joy and satisfaction, but sadly we reach a point—no, we drive ourselves to a point—where those moments are the exception and not the rule. Savoring pace is about making the knowing-that-you-are-thoroughly-alive moments the rule.

To savor is to taste or smell with pleasure, to relish, to delight in, to enjoy with pleasure. The word has its origination in the Latin *sapere,* which means "taste" and "be wise." The connection has never been more important.

For me, the savoring is in the slowing but just as much in the showing within the slowing; it is in the richer, brighter life that opens up to us once we slow down enough to notice more. Savoring pace challenges our frenzied living of paying attention to more with a gentle yet persistent appeal to pay more attention.

Savoring is relishing. The etymology of "relishing" is rich in meaning for the concept of savoring pace. "Relax," "release," and "relish" all derive from the Latin *relaxare*, "to loosen." "Relish" comes from the Old French *relais*, having to do with loosening. The taste meaning of "relish" comes from the idea of what remains in the mouth after the substance has been swallowed. Savoring pace is about loosening our overly stressed lives. It is about having the time to taste and retaste the reality of life.

Keeping the Pace

I believe that the quality of the remainder of my earthly life will be greatly determined by how well I am able to keep the savoring pace. The late pastor and politician Adam Clayton Powell Jr. had a pet phrase, "Keep the faith, baby." I've come to believe that savoring pace must be kept, as in delightfully, but tenaciously held on to. One of the reasons why we must "keep the pace, baby" is a reality called entrainment.

In *Timeshifting*, Stephen Rechtschaffen defines entrainment as a "process that governs how various rhythms fall into sync with one another." For example, if you were to place two out-of-sync pendulum clocks next to one another, guess what? You're right: in a short time, they would be exactly in sync. Rechtschaffen makes the case in his book that a parallel reality holds true with persons in relationship with each other and persons in relationship to institutions. We unconsciously catch each other's pace; we fall in step with each other's strides. Thus, if everyone around you is moving fast, rarely resting and never stopping, the likelihood of your doing the same is inevitable, unless you consciously notice, resist, and intentionally begin to live at a savoring pace.

The Biggest Foe of All

There is a major foe that you must face and defy if you are to live at a savoring pace. This major foe is you. In listening to myself and others through the years, I have come to one big conclusion: the greatest hindrance to eliminating busyness and drivenness is a mindset locked on measuring life solely in terms of production and speed. More! More! Faster! Faster!

We have been living this way so long that it's hard to admit its negative effects, even when we are hurting all over. Moreover, we have fed and have been fed by overload for so long that in a way it's taken a life of its own. Having grown stronger and stronger inside of us through the years, the overload spirit now believes it has a right to exist, and it will not give up without a fight. It will struggle hard to remain a fixture in your life, feeding off of and feeding your need for acceptance and achievement. When challenged it will point the finger at other realities in your life as the cause of your feeling down, even daring to suggest that you are not working nearly hard enough. And then there is the slick trick that dupes you into believing all is well. The overload spirit will pretend to give in to your demands for respite and play as if to say, "Okay, you got me." But the catch is, you will hear tasks teasing and taunting you throughout the supposed rest, and too often this rest is ended after only a couple of days, just long enough for the needle to move ever so slightly off of E. After this false rest we proceed to restart the engine of overloaded living and begin driving harder and faster than before to catch up on the work that has piled up. So much for the rest.

I think that there is a self inside us all that's tired of the violence we are inflicting on it, and in the words of the late legendary civil rights activist Fannie Lou Hamer, this weary and worn self is "sick and tired of being sick and tired." It is the self that Martin Luther King Jr. heard speaking in the trying days of the Montgomery bus boycott: "Almost every week—having to make so many speeches, attend so many meetings, meet so many people, write so many articles, counsel with so many groups—I face the frustration of feeling in the midst of so many things to do I am not doing anything well." There is a side of all of us that knows, even yearns for, engagement but not at the expense of wellness. It is the self that speaks to us in those quiet moments, challenging us to stop carrying so much and to slow down. Listen to the other voice within, the neglected voice; it is trying to save you. *Let it.*

Voluntary Incarceration

Perhaps you have heard the story of a certain breed of monkey that was once trapped by a simple but effective method. Hunters placed a scented food in a container to attract the animals. The monkeys would have to reach into the container to get the food. One problem that the unsuspecting monkeys could not figure out led to their capture. While the hole of the container was large enough to allow passage of a reaching hand, it was not large enough to allow a clenched fist to pass back out. Having grasped the food, the monkeys would not release it even though it meant not being able to withdraw their hand from the container. Voluntarily immobilized, they became easy prey for the hunters.

It seems that many of us are similarly enslaved in today's world. There are things that have us bound, precisely because we are holding on to them. Our incarceration is created by our clinging.

To our detriment, we cling to overloaded schedules. One of the hardest things for many of us to admit is our tendency to overdo. We can always make room for a few more tasks; we can always find a way to satisfy the requirements of additional, pressing, necessary demands. And, if we have a track record for getting the job done, what I call the curse of the competent kicks in: the more you do well, the more you will be asked to do.

There is no easy dislocation from this entrapment when much of our doing is on behalf of others or is perceived as essential to our vocational commitments. But for me, focusing on tasks only is akin to those monkeys holding on to the food. The food becomes the focus of an exclusive fixation. Of course, the problem—in the case of the monkeys—was not the food. The problem was the relationship that the animals established with the food. Laudable tasks, tempting inducements aren't the problem for overdoers; how we interpret and respond to those tasks is. We must begin to understand that doing too much and going too fast, no matter how fulfilling the task, is a matter of life and death.

Exercises

1. Choose to do three things that will help to eliminate hurry from your life. Monitor your progress on living out these choices. Once your life practice begins to reflect these new choices, move on to other choices. Don't stop until peace replaces hurry as a norm of your life.

2. Have a conversation with your deeper self. Write down all the reasons your soul and body give you for slowing down. How impassioned are the pleas? Pay attention to your response. Do you find that you are resistant to slowing down, even to your soul's plea, to God's plea? Keep returning to this dialogue until you are comfortable that you are more and more practicing peace instead of pressure in your life.

7

seeing more clearly

"I find that I notice [my family] more."
—Michael Landon

"He looked at people with generous eyes."
—Rev. Charles Adams,
eulogizing Rev. Anthony C. Campbell

"The work will wait while you show the child the rainbow, but the rainbow won't wait while you do the work."
—Author unknown

AS I BEGIN TO WRITE, THERE IS A MARVELOUS PICTURE through the midsized window to my left. It is 6:30 in the morning, and the sun's rays are adorning the small forest across the street like blinking lights on a Christmas tree. The spots of light against the shaded bark, the sheen and gleam of the early morning light on the dew-drenched leaves make for a attractive appearance of the new day. What makes this even more striking is that two weeks ago this view was not possible. The leaves had not arrived back from their winter vacation. But now, this first week of May, the leaves are back and basking in the glow of a welcoming sun.

The first calling of living at a savoring pace, seeing more clearly, has three distinct yet interrelated dimensions: seeing slowly, seeing reflectively, and seeing gratefully.

Seeing Slowly

Seeing more clearly is about holding sightings with our physical eyes (if we are not physically blind) for just a few moments longer. Two or three seconds can make all the difference in the world in a race; two or three seconds more of focused attention can make new worlds in life. I call attending to things longer with our physical sight slow seeing or elongated seeing.

Jesus practiced slow seeing a great deal, which often led to astonishing results. For example, one famous Gospel narrative has a child with a small picnic lunch saving the day. When the disciples looked at the lad, they saw him as living proof of the scarcity of food amid the crowd that had gathered to hear Jesus. They looked too quickly. Jesus, however, looked at the child longer. He saw his innocence; he saw his potential; he saw his anticipation; he saw the Holy. The result was a memorable miracle of abundance making. If Jesus had merely glanced at the child, barely noticing him, then the miracle would not have happened. The lavish miracle is due to the lavish looking, the extravagant seeing.

One of the negative consequences of our fast living is that we tend to do everything fast, including seeing fast. Because of the rush and crush of modern life, we resist holding things in our vision for extended periods of time. We don't think to see slowly; we can't afford to; we believe we may miss something important if we stand looking in one spot too long. Thus, we have cultivated the habit of seeing in a hurry, looking on the fly. The only problem is that in trying to see everything at the same time, we have ended up not truly seeing anything at all much of the time. Life has become a blurred procession of colorless images devoid of meaning and vitality.

Sometimes the results of seeing too fast are overtly dramatic and tragic, as in the instance of looking too fast at an intersection and not seeing a rapidly approaching car. But seeing fast affects us negatively in hundreds of covert, less dramatic ways on a regular basis. For example, we may look directly at family and friends and in the haste of fast seeing and the haze of easy familiarity, not *see* them, not *notice* them. The result may not be as visibly horrific as fatalities in an automobile accident, but there are fatalities: "the walking dead," people who are alive but not living, people who are looking but not seeing, hearing but not listening. I ask you, how horrible is that?

Simply holding sightings in our vision for a few seconds longer can produce a windfall of riches, including truly beholding everyday realities that are all around us. How often have you looked for something for ten minutes, twenty minutes, or longer, only to discover the item was in front of you? It was there all along within reach. No doubt you saw it several times, but you were looking past it. We look past a lot of good stuff every day.

When we look too fast or don't look enough, the consequences can be embarrassingly painful. In his autobiography, *Just As I Am,* legendary evangelist Billy Graham confesses an unforgettable, humbling experience during one of his early revival campaigns:

> And there was still another concern: my family and the personal price they were paying while I was in Los Angeles. Ruth's sister and brother-in-law, Rosa and Don Montgomery, came from New Mexico to join us for the closing week, bringing Anne, who had been staying with them. "Whose baby is this?" I asked when I saw the child in Rosa's arms, not recognizing my own daughter.[1]

A dear friend passed away during the writing of this manuscript. The Rev. Anthony C. Campbell was a gifted preacher and scholar. Rev. Charles Adams began his soul-stirring eulogy by ascribing to Tony a unique attribute I shall never forget. Said Adams, "Tony looked at people with generous eyes." As I write this, I am staring at the stately picture that graces the funeral program. Adams is telling the truth. Another way of referring to slow seeing is to say that it is beholding life with generous eyes.

The things we see by noticing more can be healing. While standing at graveside at Tony's burial, I began to bow my head and close my eyes for the Lord's Prayer. I was stopped in my movement by the glimpse of a large bird flying above. I imagined that the bird was drawn as much by the prayer as it was by the crowd. I kept my eyes on the bird throughout the prayer. As if on sacred cue, it started to fly away just as the prayer was ending. In the moment, a friend's sudden death was translated into a brother's flying away home.

Seeing Reflectively

Slow seeing, yielding a few extra seconds to things that we see on purpose or things that graciously catch our eyes, sets off the second stage of seeing more clearly: seeing with heart and mind wide open. This second stage of seeing more clearly is about opening ourselves up to the observations, questions, and conclusions inspired by those extra moments of looking. It does not mean that we spend all of our waking hours pondering the mundane. It does mean that we allow space for intervals of insight that may, on a smaller scale, provide momentary levity for living, or on a much larger scale, provide the scaffolding for a new living paradigm, a new way of envisioning and interpreting the world.

Seeing reflectively is seeing alertly and interpretively, with a learning disposition. John Steinbeck is reported to have said, "Genius is a child chasing a butterfly up a mountain." Seeing reflectively is characterized by wonder and openness about much of, if not all of, life. Seeing reflectively is seeing with pursuit in it. See reflectively is seeing with stretching, with reaching, and with grasping for new knowledge in it.

I experience this powerfully as small, innocent sightings that explode the extraordinary out of the ordinary. For instance, one morning I sat at a drive-thru window awaiting a cup of coffee. In my front peripheral vision, I saw movement. When I looked up, I saw a gentleman walking along. This darkly hued man, his morning refreshment in hand, was making his way through the parking lot. As I watched him, I noticed his walk. He was, as we used to refer to it, walking hip. He had a hip stride, leaning forward with every other step. His gait was a combination strut/march/dance. I began thinking, whatever would happen that day, he was going into it, leaning into it. He had his own living rhythm. Whatever songs life would play for him that day, life would have to play them against his striding melody established that morning. That happened several years ago, yet that man's walking witness continues to pleasantly challenge the way I journey into each new day.

Sometimes reflections will come rushing at you. At other times, sightings may not appear to be particularly revealing. But often, if you tarry just a moment, you'll find the wait to be worth it. A sighting can promote understanding about theoretical and practical concerns, directly, and perhaps just as importantly, indirectly. By indirectly, I mean that merely having our minds diverted to something else can give us the space we need to move ahead on a problem we have been pondering to the point of coming to a dead end. That's why many writers and thinkers are walkers and wanderers. Deeper understanding about a matter often comes while we are observing something altogether different.

Taking the time to really observe something, to really see it, can trigger a series of connections that may produce clarity where there was confusion. Important scientific insights have been delivered by reflective viewing—for example, gravity being discerned by Isaac Newton in the free fall of an apple. Barbara McClintock, extraordinary pioneer in modern genetics and winner of a Nobel Prize in 1983, was once asked what had enabled her to see far and deep into the mysteries of genetics. The questioner, Evelyn Fox Keller, records McClintock's amazing response: "Over and over again she tells us one must have time to look, the patience to 'hear what the material has to say to you, the openness to let it come to you.' Above all, one must have a feeling for the organism."

According to McClintock, her discoveries and her delight in them were directly related to her capacity for observation. What if we projected this kind of attitude to the matters of everyday life?

Reflecting more on what we see may remind us of important realities in life, realities we regularly undervalue or ignore. On a Sunday afternoon drive, I once observed two elderly persons and two children on a snowy mound. The kids were snowboarding down the small hill and the persons I assumed were their grandparents were cheering them on. I was instantly impressed with the joy that was so visible. As I passed them, I slowed and kept them in my rearview mirror for a moment longer. I began to marvel at the intergenerational frolicking. The final thing I thought about was that though most Sunday morning worship services had concluded, holy things were still going on. Holiness is not confined to edifices at a designated hour but may be experienced throughout all of life at any place and at any time. Moreover, while I have forgotten many sermons (many of them my own) without going overboard to remember, I have never forgotten the strangers in the snow that Sunday. I never knew their names; I have forgotten their faces. I remember their laughter, their joy. I say this not to denigrate sermonizing but to highlight the divine scenes being played out around us all the time.

Seeing Gratefully

During his bout with cancer, actor Michael Landon was asked to comment on his feelings about his family. Landon explained that while he'd always loved his family, the sickness made him "notice them more." I sense in

Landon's words the spirit of seeing the world around us, including loved ones dearest to us, with gratitude, with a grateful attitude.

In some respects, if you develop the capacity to see more slowly and reflectively, seeing gratefully will happen naturally. Sightings and insights that result from taking just a little more time to notice become joy stirrers and gratitude makers inside of us.

Though gratitude may naturally flow out from more careful observation, there is something to be said for bringing gratitude to the seeing process. That is, it is not just a matter of becoming grateful for the things we see but it is also having eyes that see gratefully. I am talking about bringing a thankful spirit to our everyday spirit. In this way, gratitude is present even before beholding an inspiring subject or experience. This is proactive thankfulness, aggressive gratitude.

There are many ways we can practice proactive thankfulness. Meditate on the blessings in your life throughout the day and not just at special occasions or on holidays; envision the possible learning opportunities at the doorway of a challenging situation; spend time reveling in the present of the new day before rushing into the presence of the new day. You will find that the more gratitude you bring to life, the more things for which you are truly grateful you will end up seeing.

Some years ago, comedian Flip Wilson was well known for playing the character Geraldine on his television show. One of Geraldine's signature statements was, "What you see is what you get!" In a very real way, what—and how—we see *is* what we get!

Really.

To live the savoring pace is to commit oneself to seeing more clearly. This means seeing slowly, reflectively, and gratefully, and seeing in these ways on purpose. It stands to reason that a lifelong, socially conditioned way of underseeing and mis-seeing is not going to be changed overnight. It will take vigilant effort on your part. Be encouraged. Seeing clearly, over and over again for the first time, is worth the effort. It is worth the effort to have eyes that, in the words of the poet Denise Levertov, "dig and burrow into the world."

Note

1. Billy Graham, *Just As I Am* (Grand Rapids, Mich.: Zondervan, 1997), 157.

Exercises

1. Perform an impromptu scan of your surroundings. You will do this by taking a minimum of eight looks: forward, left, right, back. The first time you look in these directions, focus on what is right in front of you. Take a moment to record some of the things you see. Now scan the four directions again, this time focusing on the background in each direction. Make another list. As you survey your list, note the thing you know you would have missed by casually glancing instead of looking with generous eyes.

2. Select one or two Scriptures with which you are somewhat familiar. First, read each of them at your normal reading pace. Pause. Now read them a second time, this time a little more slowly, carefully observing the punctuation marks and the spaces between the words. What new meanings did you hear the second time around?

3. Study a picture. Any picture will do. Look the first time, and note some of the things you see. Pause. Look again, paying close attention to finer details and aspects of the picture you did not see the first time.

8

listening more carefully

"It is not the ear that hears, it is not the physical organ that performs that act of receptivity. It is the total person who hears."
—M. C. Richards, *Centering*

"For there is no greater way to depersonalize another than to speak to him without also listening."
—Houston Smith, *The Religions of Man*

SO OFTEN WE HEAR WITHOUT TRULY LISTENING, WITH-out paying caring attention to what we are hearing. What makes listening so difficult? One reason may be that there are so many sounds out there. How do we know which ones to listen to and which ones to ignore? Most of us go on automatic pilot and feign attention to as many sounds as we can, as opposed to going through the more demanding task of discerning between sounds. Another thing that makes lis-tening difficult these days is that from the time we get up in the morning to the time we go to bed at night we are prompted to live fast. Real listening has patience inside of it; it cannot be hurried. Hurry is not a good listening posture.

Whatever the cause, listening-less living is impoverished living. Too much is missed and lost when we do not give soulful ear (a word lodged at the center of the heart) to the sounds and silence around us—too much that can make a difference in the way we live our lives.

Voices

What difference does a voice make? Take a moment to imagine a friend calling your name. Hear the friend's voice call out to you several times. Now imagine a loved parent, grandparent, or guardian calling your name. Same name, different voice, different emotional reactions from within.

Our voices are amazing, multipurpose instruments. Through our voices we announce initially as infants and continue to announce as adults our personhood to the world. Our voices often give us away: our most authentic self and our true feelings. If someone is able to read your voice, that person can read you. Our voices carry the depths of our delight and our pains. We know soaring and sorrow from the sounds that rise up and out. Through our voices we surrender and we take a stand. Our voices carry our praises, our curses, and the majority of matters in between.

In the garden after Jesus' resurrection, Mary sees a stranger she believes to be a cemetery attendant. Who else would be in the graveyard so early in the morning but someone who was obligated to be there? In her mind, the stranger was a laborer working the morning shift. Nothing about his appearance or the presence he exuded suggested otherwise. Not until the stranger raised his voice and called out her name did Mary realize that she was in the company of one raised from the dead. Jesus' voice gave him away. Mary recognized Jesus by his voice. In all the world, in all her world, there was no other voice like it.

The phrase "hearing voices" is generally regarded in a negative light. While we usually link the words to persons who are mentally unstable, really listening to voices for the first time can be the entryway to richer communication and living. What's worse? Hearing what we are not supposed to hear, or not hearing what we are supposed to hear? When it comes to voices, which ones should you be paying more attention to? Which voices, though they perhaps do not demand it, deserve more attention than they are presently receiving?

Noises

The very word *noise* has an uninviting quality to it. Noise is intrusive; it is sound gone awry. Hearing a strange noise at night more often than not springs us to alert, if not alarm. When children have gone from the happy land of tolerable play to the troubling territory of free-fall tumult, adults cry out, "Cut out all that noise!" Yet savoring pace challenges us to search out the value imbedded in some, if not many, of the noises we hear.

One morning I sat down to begin my period of devotion. Usually I start with a period of attending to the silence. When I am done, the silence remains as a soothing background melody to my journaling and inspirational reading. On this morning, seconds into my initial celebration of silence, I was jarred by the sound of the dryer in the next room. When I asked my wife—ever so delicately—why the dryer had to be on so early in the morning, she told me that one of our children needed the clothes inside, including tennis shoes, that day. I had no choice; the noise would have to continue. I tried to make the best of a bad situation. Gradually grace came in the form of hearing blessings in the noise. As I listened to the dryer, including those shoes bouncing back and forth, the noise became signs of a devoted mother and a healthy child. I began to thank God for my caring wife and our four demanding but no less delightful children. The noise turned into a song of blessing that solicited an unscheduled morning prayer of gratitude from me.

Nature

As I write this, I am hearing the wind blowing through the leaves of the large tree in front of our home and the large chorus of trees across the street. What does the sound do for me? Why does it appeal to me so? I believe part of the attraction has to do with the mystery of it all. Though I am familiar with the scientific rationale that explains the wind, I do not—and do not ever want to—believe there is any explanation that discloses the full essence of the wind. When I hear the wind blowing, I hear a reality that is an escape artist when it comes to our being able to explain its meaning and might.

And then there is the soothing. Not always does the wind soothe the leaves outside. When fall arrives, winds with a different calling will carry these same leaves to their deaths. Next, winter winds will come and unapologetically rush through and by bare tree limbs. This morning's wind is not threatening or menacing. Its sound is cordial, compelling even. As opposed to saying, "Make way" or "Get out of the way," I hear the wind saying, "It is well." I listen, and for a moment I fly with the wind, feeling the truth of its decree for my life.

The other of nature's sounds even more memorizing for me than the wind is the sound of trickling water. I know I am not the only one enraptured by this sound. Pieces of art that feature water trickling down are growing in popularity, as are tapes and compact disks that carry the sound of falling water with and without musical accompaniment. A most cherished memory from my Alaskan vacation a few years ago is waters rolling down the mountainsides and cascading beneath foot bridges.

What can I say other than after first stopping me, the movement of the water moves my spirit? I may have several unconscious influences here. Perhaps the sound of waters circling and stopping and running takes me back to those first sounds heard in my mother's womb. In my black Baptist church tradition, baptismal water is a source and vessel of spiritual transformation. Moreover, as a boy preacher I grew up hearing as well as repeating biblical water pronouncements such as, "He leads me beside still waters" (Psalm 23:2), "let justice roll down like waters, and righteousness like an everflowing stream" (Amos 5:24), and "those who drink of the water that I will give them will never be thirsty" (John 4:14). We sang, usually at baptisms, "Take me to the water," and "Wade in the water." When I hear water I hear transcendence, hallowed beyond-ness.

What of nature's many sounds most moves you? How might you learn to listen even more intently to those sounds waiting to be heard again for the first time, and to those sounds that you and I have yet to hear for the first time?

Music

Ella Fitzgerald, the jazz singer who musical genius Duke Ellington said was "beyond category," brought me to new depths of musical appreciation. It was a Saturday night, and I was feeling down, way down. My predicament worsened every time I thought about the unprepared sermon that I had to preach the next morning. Then came grace. I began listening to a CD I had not heard before, entitled *The Intimate Ella.* It featured the great vocalist with Paul Smith at the piano. The next fifty minutes or so had a profoundly transforming impact on my life. In a moment that found me in the valley of despair, it wasn't just *what* Ella Fitzgerald sang ("I Cried for You," "Then You've Never Been Blue," "Misty," and "Reach for Tomorrow," to name a few of the selections) but *how* she sang them. She caressed each song lyric; every word mattered to her and increasingly to me. And into each word she poured a drop or two of honey that became for me a sweet source of soulful encouragement. She sang in such a way as to *make my heart hear her.* I have played that CD many times since then. Each time I find myself listening with soft vigilance to her every word.

Howard Mandel once wrote about a particular Miles Davis rendition: *"In a Silent Way* draws me in, holds me close, turns my ear to its arcs, planes and tangents. I've always found it beautiful, and it's helped me to listen to everything else for 30 years."[1] I share Mandel's belief about jazz music in general. Listening to it, its dancing, prancing, bowing, bending, soaring notes have enhanced my overall listening to life. And the thrill of hearing the beloved sound of a particular selection is surpassed only by the thrill of hearing an attractive alien note I have never heard before.

Words

In a time when we are overwhelmed by words from the moment we wake up to the moment we go to bed at night, words may be the hardest of all to listen to. We wake up to the words of our first mental thoughts and ruminations. Then, for some of us, it's on to attending to the words of our devotional lives, our loved ones, and the media. As we make it out into the world, whether driving or traveling by another means of transportation, chances are that words surround you via signs and billboards most of the time. All of this before undertaking the word responsibilities of our vocational tasks. Perhaps learning how to *not* listen to words is the more necessary skill to cultivate today.

At a time when we are experiencing word overload (what one writer calls "verbal intoxication"), how do we begin to listen more carefully to words? Perhaps the place to begin is by understanding that words are not the problem; the problem is our casual, careless use of words. As we begin to believe this, maybe we will be encouraged to choose and say our words more carefully, to avoid the double talk of cloaking lies and the fast talk of scampering away from the truth. Maybe we can resist the quick speech of deep-thought avoidance and the boisterous speech of bullying domination. The first step in learning how to listen to words more carefully is mustering the determination to speak more delicately and carefully, not in the sense of walking on eggs but in the sense of handling precious gems. The words we hear will begin to matter more when the words we say begin to matter more. How will you know if your speech patterns are changing? By listening to yourself.

Silence

Many of us are uncomfortable with silence. This may have something to do with the many negative meanings attached to silence. Too much silence in a household including two or more children means that they are up to something. Often punishment of children is communicated through the rhetoric of silencing: "Sit over there, and don't say a word." "Go to your room, and I better not here a sound out of you." As adults we learn how to harden disagreement by giving each other the silent treatment. Silence is often associated with diminished mental and verbal ability. Students who do not speak up in class are perceived as slow, and acquaintances or co-workers who speak minimally in conversations are perceived as uninformed. Speaking of conversations, pauses are notoriously difficult for us to handle, especially if the dialogue involves three or more people. Suddenly finding ourselves stripped of our chatter, if only for a moment, we feel embarrassed, naked.

One of our biggest problems with silence is that it smacks of nonproductivity. How many times have you tried to relax for a moment only to have your peace aborted by the nagging cry of something that needed to be done? Were it the task alone, perhaps you would be able to hold onto rest more easily. But there is usually another cry more difficult to resist, the one that has you feeling guilty about taking time off when there is still so much work to be done. Because we measure ourselves mostly in terms of what we do, the silence of not doing can be fiercely threatening.

Perhaps the most troubling aspect of silence is that sometimes it facilitates our hearing things we do not want to hear. Do you remember being alone in an empty house when you were a child? Or being unable to go to sleep in the middle of the night in a house that was still and silent? Oh, the things we heard or thought we heard and did not want to hear. The silence can be even more foreboding for adults. David writes in Psalm 39:2, "I was silent and still; I held my peace to no avail; my distress grew worse."

If we are to listen more to the silences, we have no other choice but to begin to formulate alternative beliefs about the silences that are formidable enough to challenge those currently reigning inside of us. There are good reasons for viewing silence as more friend than foe.

The Bible is a good place to start. In its pages, silence, often communicated as "stillness," is associated with wisdom (Psalm 4:4; Proverbs 17:27-28), the recovery of physical and emotional strength (Isaiah 40:31), and a deeper apprehension of God (Psalm 46:10). I know that I have benefited from silence in these three ways, particularly in regard to a continuing, if not deepening, relationship with God.

Though silence does not take all of the mystery out of God, it can on occasion make the mystery less daunting and more inviting. I recall one of my morning devotions a week after September 11, 2001. I seemed to be in a fog mentally and spiritually. Though I sat in stillness, stillness did not sit in me. I felt deeply troubled by the new intensity of evil unleashed in our world, by the reality of thousands of lives lost and the many more thousands of grieving family and friends left. Moreover, I remember being teased and taunted by nagging vocational realities and concerns. So there was all this nonsilence in the silence.

91

In this mixture, I began to speak the credo I try to repeat in my mind three or four times each morning: "I am a child of God, a person who God loves unconditionally. I will live and laugh, give and grow, in God's love at a savoring pace." I did not complete three or four expressions of the credo that morning. In fact, I did not finish saying it once. I stumbled the first time over the second phrase. In the silence, I clearly heard the error. In the silence of my un-silence, I kept hearing the error echoing in my mind. It stirred inside of me deep reflecting about the meaning and mandate of my mistake. Instead of saying, "a person who God loves unconditionally," I said, "a person who loves God unconditionally."

I heard my misthought as soon as it rolled out of my mind, and immediately I felt it challenging me. It began questioning my alleged affection for God and the grounds on which it was based. Did I love God unconditionally? Was I able to think kindly toward God in the face of new and ferocious evil? Could I feel tenderness for God in the middle of threatening circumstances and conditions? Could I trust God in light of what appeared to be the absence of God's protective hand? After a while, the questions gave way to a reassuring request that mediated welcome serenity: "Trust me."

Note

1. Howard Mandel, "Electric Miles," *Schwann Inside Jazz & Classical,* Vol. 2, No. 9, September 2001, 23.

Exercises

1. Gather three different versions of the same song. Carefully listen to each. In what ways are they similar? In what ways are they different?

2. Do a sound scan. Take a few moments to note every sound you hear over the next five minutes.

3. Ask two or three friends you speak with on a frequent basis to inform you when you cut them off in conversation.

4. As you participate in conversations over the next few days, pay close attention to how frequently persons interrupt each other.

9

thinking more deeply

"*Sometimes you need to sit and think. Sometimes you need to just sit.*"
— Satchel Page

"*In contrast to hypervigilance, which locks in an object of attention, soft vigilance remains open to novelty.*"
— Ellen Langer

"*By reinterpreting reality and begetting novelty, we keep from becoming rigid.*"
— Stephen Nachmanovitch

I DEFINE THINKING MORE DEEPLY AS HAVING A searching soul, continually being on the lookout for new insight and understanding. Thinking more deeply is not just a matter of accumulating more information about subjects to the point of knowing them, as we say, inside out. Also, as laudable a goal as it may be, thinking more deeply is more than arriving at certain indisputable bedrock truths about life. Intellectual accumulation and thoughtful certainty smack of acquisition, accomplishment, having arrived. In my mind, thinking more deeply is the opposite. It is an active sense of never having fully acquired, accomplished, or arrived regarding anything.

Openness Before the New

In chapter 3, verses 1-21 of John's Gospel, there is a record of a remarkable encounter between Jesus and a religious leader named Nicodemus. In this passage, we stand to learn as much from Nicodemus as we do from Jesus, although Jesus is doing most of the talking. Jesus is talking so much because Nicodemus keeps asking him questions: "How can anyone be born after having grown old?" "Can one enter a second time into the mother's womb and be born?" "How can these things be?" These are the questions we know about. Given the urgent matters being discussed and the intensity of the exchange, it is easy to believe that Nicodemus asked many more questions.

This text is a picture of someone caught in the act of thinking more deeply, and it allows us to see some of what is involved in the process. Though Nicodemus knows a great deal, his known does not keep him from pursuing the unknown. What is even more amazing is that though Nicodemus is a credentialed religious educator, his learned status has not dissolved his curiosity, his openness to new possibilities. Moreover, he is open and vulnerable with someone who does not have the standing in the community that he has.

Nicodemus's exploration of new knowledge is not limited by cultural and class bias. Perhaps the most inspiring element of the conversation between Jesus and Nicodemus is that it has no real conclusion. The chapter continues with a discussion regarding Jesus and John the Baptist. But you do not get the sense that Jesus and Nicodemus are through. Their conversation is left hanging. Jesus makes a summary declaration of sorts that evokes no recorded response from Nicodemus. Perhaps upon hearing it Nicodemus has questions at the ready; maybe he even asks them. We do not hear them. Neither do we hear any formal good-byes. Jesus and Nicodemus may have ceased talking, but their conversation is far from over. That is the feeling I have at the end of verse 21.

Likewise, thinking more deeply is a neverending affair. It is always ongoing. It is being in diligent, disturbing, delightful search of Truth, wherein we are whole and free.

Kissing the Mystery

Thinking deeply does not mean thinking harder. In fact, thinking deeply, at precious tender places, means not thinking at all.

Allow me to share a final morning devotional experience with you. This particular morning, I was having a tougher time than usual attaining a mental stillness I enjoy touching at the beginning of each day. This morning, mental stillness was especially elusive. One thought after another crowded into my mind. They were not monumental but rather mundane thoughts, including wondering where I had misplaced my comb or who had taken it. The procession of the trivial continued to the point where there were too many to manage, and I gave in. I decided that it would take more energy to stop thinking that morning than I wanted to expend. I would spend the morning pondering small things. Though there is no small value in that, to my surprise and wonder, suddenly I began to receive and record curious impressions challenging my easy surrender to continued thinking:

Do not give into thinking so easily. Remember that your thoughts, no matter how profound and engaging (or miniscule and uninspiring) are always limited. God is always beyond thinking about God. Life is always something more than your most rigorous comprehending of it. As helpful as thinking is, you must always remember that it is never fully revelatory. It is always limited and constricted by your limits and constrictions. At the extreme worst, thinking can be used to stave off encountering truth.

So, do not give up your pursuit of soul quiet, sanctified nonthought, so quickly. What right have you to believe that the things of God and life are apprehended through thought alone? Thinking can cover only so much of the territory that is truth. Thinking has no monopoly on truth. Much of truth's vast expanse is traversed best through mental surrender. Often thinking, especially exclusive and fixated thinking, obstructs genuine enlightenment.

Do not give up so easily your pursuit of the rested mind. The mind at ease is often more welcoming of the truth that sets you free. The apprehension of God is not just a matter of thinking. It is a matter of being open, vulnerable, and even lost deliberately and on purpose. It is a matter of surrendering to unimagined strengthening, God's, and, surprise of surprises, your own.

I have come across proofs for the impressions I was graced with that morning. Almost every book I have read about creative persons and creativity has mentioned the important place that nothingness plays in the creative process. Many scientists testify that significant breakthroughs often occur to them precisely when they are not actively thinking about the problem under consideration. Writers speak of having their literary juices stirred by performing tasks that have nothing to do with stitching words together. Some musicians keep notebooks or tape reorders on their nightstands in order to capture ideas and concepts that come to them in the dancing of their dreams. Sermon segments have been handed to me while I'm conversing with strangers standing in the supermarket checkout line, and sometimes while just standing. The mind at ease is no less capable of registering remarkable insights than the mind that is intentionally and actively engaged. Our challenge is not to denigrate the latter but to notice and appreciate more the former.

As for the reasons behind the comparable formidableness of the engaged and rested mind, I know none. I am content with living with and in the mystery and on occasion even kissing it.

The brilliant Albert Einstein said, "The most beautiful thing we can experience is the mysterious."

Being Saved from Deathly Knowing

Thinking more deeply rescues us from deathly knowing. Deathly knowing is closed knowing. It is the knowledge hardened to the point of being an obstruction to new learning.

Martha is the unsung heroine of John 11, the story of the resurrection of Lazarus. Throughout the story she evidences a childlike, compelling capacity for open knowing: knowing always ending with a comma, never a period. For example, though Jesus' tardiness may have been a factor in Lazarus's death, Martha knows, according to verse 22, that even now God will give whatever Jesus asks. And her open knowing is visible again. Though she knows that resurrection is reserved for the last day, she is open to Jesus' startling and striking new knowing in verse 25: "I am the resurrection and the life. Those who believe in me, even though they die, will live, and everyone who lives and believes in me will never die. Do you believe this?"

Martha does not say, "That's preposterous" and walk off. She does not say, "I am sad, not insane." She does not think to herself, "Resurrection and life, he's good but not that good." Rather, she lets his words in. They tingle inside. And she wades out into the cool, refreshing waters of new knowing.

Howard Thurman once prayed:

Keep alive in me the forward look, the high hope,
The onward surge
   [the root of our word *resurrection*].
Let me not be frozen
Either by the past or the present.
Grant me, O patient Father, Thy sense of the future
Without which all life would sicken and die.[1]

Note

1. Howard Thurman's prayer "Oh God, I Need Thee" (1951), in *Conversations with God: Two Centuries of Prayers by African Americans,* ed. James Melvin Washington (New York: Harper-Perennial, 1994), 183.

Exercises

1. Rediscover the child in you who used to ask, "Why?" Asking questions is a regular, effective way of expanding your mental boundaries. Ask questions as you read, as you listen to the news, as you work, as you relate with others, as you journey through life.

2. Here is a fun way to think more deeply that I accidentally stumbled upon. One day, in a moment of soft silliness, I said to my son, "You know what they say, 'What goes around, may be lost.'" We both laughed. The next day I gave him another playful derivation, "What goes around will make you dizzy if you keep looking at it." This went on for about a month. It dawned on me that this game was a way of practicing thinking about something familiar in unfamiliar ways. Practicing thinking differently helps us to think more deeply, more naturally. Think of a familiar expression. How many new humorous endings can you create for it? Who says thinking can't be delightful?

3. Begin paying attention to how your mind is changing on some issues, the ways you are becoming new day by day. Noticing your evolving spirit and mind is a way of nurturing positive transformation.

10

savoring pace life lines

"Beauty remains, even in misfortune. If you look for it, you discover more and more happiness and you regain your balance."
—Anne Frank, *The Diary of a Young Girl*

SELF-COACHING IS ESSENTIAL TO LIVING AT A SAVORING pace. One of the ways I coach myself is to develop memorable statements that counter the cues to move faster that we all get constantly. My statements are countercues; I call them Savoring Pace Lines. I started out by writing these cues on index cards and reading a new one each day. This led to my creating a fifty-card collection to help others change their living pace, one thought at a time. For the past two years I have also published a weekly Savoring Pace Life Line Reflection each Monday morning at www.savoring-pace.com. Both the cards and the Reflection are tangible small big ways to initiate behavioral transformation. They are manageable ways of claiming your power over the destructive forces of hurry and overload.

Here are fourteen Life Line reflections that I hope will assist you further in realizing your alternative sacred pace in a speeding world.

Practice Defiant Gratitude

Anne Frank's amazing words and the testimonies of other courageous spirits who have withstood this world's worst face testify to the impossible possibility of defiant gratitude: the ability to savor sweetness while suffering.

It is necessary to regularly practice defiant gratitude in our delightful but dangerous world if we are to journey on in hope and not be crushed to the earth and then under it by despair.

One important key, it seems, to living this miracle is choosing. Defiant gratitude is not simply given to us, nor do we merely stumble upon it. No, this kind of gratitude, more than any other kind, is intentionally and defiantly grasped by the human spirit. Of course, the strength to grab is given by the dogged God who cries tenacious tears of grace and love amid and against all hell has or ever will have to offer.

Welcome Each New Day

I am a planner. I plan my tomorrows. I dream about and plan for the future, including the future that I perceive afar in the distance. I can remember sitting in high school classes planning my college and seminary years. In seminary, I spent a good deal of time charting doctoral program timetables and strategies.

Though being the consummate planner has helped me, through the years I have had an increasing nagging sensation about its having hurt me. Now there is with me a cloud, more company than threat, which tells me this: Be careful that you do not fixate your thoughts so on the future that you are unable to give the present the focused attention that it deserves. I am haunted by what I may have missed as a high school student when I too often left the learning that was near me to saunter off as I sped more than a mile up the road. It is possible to miss today's blessings in pursuit of tomorrow's bounty.

Plan, yes, but within, not apart from, the vast wealth of today. Each new day and experience is filled with manifold blessings, some blatant, others hidden. As you envision your future, do so in full view of today. Frederick Buechner is as right as right can be when he declares, "All other days have either disappeared into darkness and oblivion or not yet emerged from them. Today is the only day there is."[1]

As you go about wandering off in the field of your future, do so with wide-eyed appreciation for the fertile terrain of today. Welcome today. Ask yourself:

What is there for me to learn today?

In what ways can I grow today?

How can I receive and share today?

What am I truly thankful for today?

Be Afraid; Don't Become Your Fears

Many persons who escaped from the World Trade Center on September 11, 2001, are still living in horror. Inez Graham made it down sixty-one flights of stairs just minutes before the first building crumbled around her. A *New York Times* reporter, Andrew Jacobs, writes about how Graham's life has crumbled:

Inez Graham is at war with her memory. She spends most of her days sobbing and afraid, battling images of flames and falling debris and trying to quell the soundtrack of screams in her head. A ringing phone, a plane overhead or a passing truck make her hunker down in fear. She refuses to go outside. She tells friends not to visit and says the smell of smoke, like some unseen phantom, lingers around her home in Newark.

She tries to stave off sleep, but when she finally dozes of, the nightmares are always the same. She is back at the World Trade Center, barefoot and breathless, trying to outrun the tidal wave of concrete and glass. But in this version, her daughters are with her, and she cannot save them. "I want the old Inez back," she said, giving in to another round of tears. "But I just can't get that day out of my head."

A photograph of Inez Graham with her best friend, Dee Howard, another survivor, accompanies their story. I am posting the picture so that I can view it every day. It will remind me to pray for Inez Graham, Dee Howard, and their many similarly wounded comrades I will never know by name or by face. My prayer for them today is that a resolve expressed by Parker Palmer becomes, in time, their absolute release: "I will always have fears, but I need not be my fears."

Just To Be Is a Blessing

This month's kitchen calendar inspiration is "Just to be is a blessing; just to live is holy." I saw it yesterday and stared at it for a moment. When I saw the name under the quote, I smiled. Abraham Heschel would say something like that. Standing, looking at the calendar, I remembered something Heschel said after the historic civil rights march in Selma: "I felt my legs were praying." Both quotes indicate that Heschel was in touch with the sacredness of life at the ground floor.

Often and innocently, we associate blessing with select acquisition and holiness with special ritual. These are penthouse definitions that lock us into believing that blessing and holiness have to do with certain extraordinary, isolated experiences. The genius of Heschel is that he discerned goodness and Godness to be constantly nearby. Heschel and his kind do not have to go far to experience deep peace and joy. In fact, they do not have to go anywhere; present being is sufficient enough holy ground.

Two thousand years ago, Jesus said, "The kingdom of God is among [within] you" (Luke 17:21). It is a striking observation, especially when you consider that conditions and prerequisites are not given. There is always something amazingly wonderful inside of us that we have nothing on earth to do with being there. It is a gift. Isn't this another reason to fathom that merely being is a blessing and just living is holy?

Side with Your Soul

Derrick Bell tells a memorable story about Alice Walker in his new book, *Ethical Ambition*. Walker had received a commission from a well-known magazine to write about her experiences growing up in the South. When the future Pulitzer Prize winner presented her article, the magazine accepted it, but with the stipulation that she make major revisions. Walker thought the recommendations went too far and said so. A standoff ensued, and

Walker was finally told in a face-to-face encounter, "Alice, you don't understand. If you want us to publish your piece, you have to make these changes." Eying her budding career but sensing what was bubbling up inside her even more, Walker stood up, picked up her manuscript, and said, "It's you who do not understand. All I have to do in life is save my soul."

The word *soul* refers to the part of us without which we would not exist. If you lost a job or a limb, though wounded, you would still be you. But if you lost your soul, your vital essence, your sacred aliveness, you would lose you. Over time, it is possible to come to hold things, such as one's history, close to heart and soul. These matters of the soul cannot be violated without doing damage to the soul. More wise than she was ambitious, Alice Walker chose to protect her soul.

There are many threats to our sacred aliveness, some obvious and indirect, others more subtle and indirect. Take the time to ponder decisions. Always side with your soul.

No Sitting; No Soaring

I'd been in the hotel room only a few minutes when I noticed two paintings of birds on the wall. I could tell from just glancing at them that they were probably painted by the same person; I was right. The paintings had a lot in common: the birds were portrayed in great detail, many colors were used, and most interesting of all to me, in both pictures the birds were perched on tree limbs.

As I stared at the images, a question popped into my head: In the artist's mind, have the birds just landed, or are they readying themselves to fly? After more careful examination, I concluded that I couldn't be certain one way or the other.

As I began to turn away from the paintings, I discovered that though I was done with them, the paintings were not done with me. Suddenly the following thought landed in my mind: Whether having flown or preparing to fly, if the birds in the picture flew without ceasing eventually they would fall to the earth in fatal exhaustion. No Sitting; No Soaring.

Just like the birds, our soaring is dependent upon our sitting. Activism and achievement are dependent upon respite and contentment.

Take Your Time

I grew up in the African American Baptist religious tradition in New Orleans. One of the historic and beloved features of my spiritual home is the talkback between congregation and minister during the preaching moment. Some liturgical-dialogical expressions are more common than others; one of the most familiar from pew to pulpit is "Take your time."

"Take your time" has multiple meanings depending upon the state of the sermon. A congregant seeking a deeper understanding may be urging the preacher to elaborate more, to furnish added information. Or, it is possible that the preacher is talking too fast and the expression "take your time" means "slow down."

There is a third possibility. Sometimes, preachers talk upon just the right words at just the right time. "Take your time" in this context means that what the preacher is saying is hitting home, is meeting a need. "Take your time" is a request for time to savor the portion given and a signal that a "second helping" (repeating a thought or phrase) would be appreciated.

There are unique moments, tasks, respites that should not be hurried. On the contrary, due to the special offering they hold for us, such experiences ought be slowed more intentionally and deliberately.

Be on the lookout for those things when you should— and more than you normally would—"take your time."

Stop Sleepwalking Through Life

Of course, when I advise you to stop sleepwalking through life, I am not talking about sleepwalking in the usual sense. Aside from physically walking in our sleep, there are other ways we can sleepwalk. For example, in his classic book on racial oppression, *Invisible Man,* Ralph Ellison refers to persons who practice racial hate and prejudice as "sleeping ones." Ellison warns that "there are few things in the world as dangerous as sleepwalkers."

There is yet another way of sleepwalking that we need to become more aware of and develop a greater resistance to: sleepwalking through Christmas. We appear to be awake at this holy time of ultimate expectancy and fulfillment through our apparent activity, but actually—sadly—too often we are asleep to the crucial matters of the heart and soul at Christmas. We end up sleepwalking—and running— right past holy ground.

In his fascinating book, *Awareness,* Anthony DeMello refers to spirituality as "waking up." His advice on being awake in life—more entirely alive—is profound and worth remembering: "In order to wake up, the one thing you need the most is not energy, or strength, or youthfulness, or even great intelligence. The one thing you need most of all is the readiness to learn something new."[2]

May you be blessed with newness of life and deep, abiding wakefulness.

Practice Divine Curiosity

Helmut Thielicke was a great theologian who was also known for his wonderful preaching ability. He concludes his autobiography, *Notes from a Wayfarer*, by explaining that learning to experience the gospel "without fear" was an important breakthrough in his spiritual maturity. But, as Thielicke proceeds in his writing, he finds "without fear" to be an insufficient description of the way he'd truly learned to engage the gospel: "Without fear? That is actually an understatement. I enter rather with the divine curiosity of a person who has discovered the new and unknown not only as something that is hidden but at the same time as something that is secure. Even that which is new and unknown rests in the peace of those hands that embrace both the past and the future."[3]

It is not enough to engage the gospel—or this new year—without fear. That's good, but according to at least one insightful theologian, we can take it one step further. We can move past not having fear to having something that is ideally rooted in a deep, abiding spiritual trust. That something may be referred to as sacred interest in all of life, or, as Thielicke identified it, "divine curiosity."

John Steinbeck is reported to have defined genius as "a child chasing a butterfly up a mountain." May you manifest in your work, play, and relationships this new year that child's spirit—the spirit of sustained divine curiosity.

You Are a Dancing Spirit

In one of my favorite pictures of Dr. Martin Luther King, he is dancing with his wife, Coretta. While in Sweden to accept

109

the 1964 Nobel Peace Prize, they attended a ball in Stockholm. In *My Life with Martin Luther King Jr.*, Coretta recalls the tension and thrill of dancing with Martin, a Baptist preacher, once again:

> We had not danced publicly since our college days in Boston. Martin had told me then that, as a Baptist, when he became pastor of a church, we would not be able to dance anymore in public because it would be distasteful to the older members of the congregation. We never had, and Martin was quite reluctant to dance now. The student committee begged and begged us, so we finally consented to waltz. It was great fun to be dancing again with Martin.[4]

The picture of Coretta and Martin King dancing, and their sacrificial work for nonviolence, justice, and unity, brings to mind words written by the legendary dancer Judith Jamison. She concludes her autobiography, *Dancing Spirit*, as follows:

> Think of movement as much bigger than what your body says you're limited to. Your hand can go into the depths of your heart to pull out what you need to communicate with another person.... Dance is bigger than the physical body. Think bigger than that. When you extend your arm, it doesn't stop at the end of your fingers, because you're dancing bigger than that; you're dancing spirit. Take a chance. Reach out. Go further than you've ever gone before.... Let your light shine.[5]

Bless Your Boats

Lucille Clifton's most recent collection of published poetry is entitled *Blessing the Boats*. *Blessing the Boats* is a poem originally from a past book treasure by this wonderful poet. The fact that the poem reappears, this time leading the procession of her new work, tells you something about the poem's persistent influence.

All of thirteen lines, the precisely selected and arranged words trumpet the value of journey in life. Life is movement—wise, nourishing respite throughout—but movement indeed, from moment to moment and place to place. Our places aren't always geographical locations. Some of our most challenging and engaging trips have to do with journeying from old ideas to new insights and from entrenched allegiances to communities in tender formation. But onward we go, if we are to let learning and growth have their way with us.

Clifton's *Blessing the Boats* invites us to a love for journey, the trips we choose to make and, perhaps, even the ones we find ourselves taking because life has said so. *Blessing the Boats* invites us, as well, to remember and honor all of the vessels that serve to transport us—all of the persons, ideas, and organizations that carry us onward "beyond the face of fear."

Receive now the blessing that is the conclusion of Clifton's poem:

… may you open your eyes to water
water waving forever
and may you in your innocence
sail through this to that.[6]

Attend To What Is Alive Inside of You

The late singer, pianist, songwriter, and arranger Donny Hathaway is one of my favorite artists. Reared in the black church, Hathaway's music resonates with pathos and passion, suffering and hope. His voice is equally and intensely loyal to the blues and "blues breakthrough" reality of everyday life. Simply put, Donny Hathaway can make you cry, and he can make you shout for joy.

Hathaway began singing on stage at the age of three with his grandmother, noted gospel singer Martha Cromwell. Back then Donny Hathaway was known as "Little Donny Pitts: The Nation's Youngest Gospel Singer." The youngster was a sensation, but, of course, the best was yet to come. In fact, the child prodigy felt something wonderfully amazing welling up inside of him. At age six, Hathaway began telling his grandmother, "You should hear the music I'm hearing in my head."

What would have happened if Hathaway had been unable to hear the music? What if he had heard the music and not noticed it, ignored it, or paid little attention to it? In order for countless others to be blessed by the artistry of Donny Hathaway, he had to first honor and trust what was coming to life inside of him, more and more.

The great teacher and spiritual advisor Howard Thurman once advised a college graduate wrestling with several vocational choices, "Do what is on fire inside of you. More than anything else, the world needs persons who are on fire."

What's most alive inside of you these days? How can you pay more attention to it? Can you allow more time in your busy schedule to hear what is calling you? Maybe it is a new calling or perhaps it is one too long suppressed and denied that, thankfully, continues to tease and taunt you.

Attend to what is alive inside of you. You are waiting; your call is waiting; and in the words of one of Donny Hathaway's most magnificent musical gifts to us all, *To Be Young, Gifted, and Black*, "There's a whole world waiting for you."

Discover the Fullness in Being Empty

My morning devotional begins with a period of silence and stillness. During this twenty- to thirty-minute period, I attempt to be empty, to avoid thinking about anything. I remember persons at my home church (Mount Hermon Baptist in New Orleans) sometimes beginning their church prayers on behalf of all gathered with the phrase, "Lord, we come before you as empty pitchers before a full fountain." Similarly, my initial devotional action is being purposefully empty.

Some days are easier than others when it comes to observing emptiness. There are few days when I am totally free from the cry of some pressing concern trying to crash in on my emptiness. When concerns press on me, I have learned to gently acknowledge the intruder and say to it, "I'll attend to you in a moment." Yet I still have those days when emptiness is too much of a losing struggle.

I persist with the practice of emptiness for several reasons. I resist beginning the day clinging to a list of things I need to get done. With all due respect to such lists, including all of the things on them that I thoroughly enjoy doing, I find that when I start out in this way, I end up living out the day as if I were a competitor in a steeplechase, performing one jump after the next. I subsequently measure the quality of the day in terms of number of things accomplished. As it happens, many of my best days occur when I dare to give undivided attention to things not on the list or to the areas of margin (the empty spaces of respite) between the words on the list. Beginning with emptiness reminds me that life is more than a list of things to do.

I begin with emptiness, also, to start my day out from a place of peace. Whatever happens on any given day, I will have experienced peace. Experiencing and establishing peace in my heart not only creates a serene starting point but also a calming checkpoint throughout the day and a familiar resting place when the day is done—a place to come home to.

There is another thing about the emptiness: there is a fullness to it. Somewhere during the time of being empty, I try to receive the refreshing infilling of God's unconditional love and acceptance. Perhaps this was the deepest yearning behind the prayer I heard as a child, "Lord, we come before you as empty pitchers before a full fountain."

Lean Into Your Power

My wife and I enjoy a brisk three-mile walk at the beginning of the day: a mile to the track, a mile at the track, and a mile back home. While at the track, we often jog the curves. That is where my two-word declaration usually kicks in: first step—"I," second step—"choose," next step—"I," following step—"choose." Around the curves I go to the mental beat of "I choose," "I choose," "I choose."

How often do you feel overwhelmed by the demands you place on yourself and those placed on you by family, friends, co-workers, and life in general? The real problem is not everything that's being asked of you but forgetting that you have the power to choose how you will respond to everything that's being asked of you. Claiming your ability to choose is the dynamic difference between your feeling pushed and pulled around all the time and your intentionally living—sometimes dancing even—to the rhythm of holy empowerment.

This brings us to a fundamental question: Who is in charge in your life?

There are many who surrender most of their power to authority figures and institutions. Though they may balk about the excessive demands placed on them by those figures and institutions, the fact is they prefer that stress to the laborious, albeit liberating, work of self-determination.

Other persons feel impotent when it comes to taking charge of their lives. They feel weakness and numbness in the face of opportunities to exert mental and verbal force. Perhaps the malady beneath the malady is named by Nelson Mandela. Exhorting a people not to break under the weight of internalized oppression, Mandela said, "Our deepest fear is not that we are inadequate. Our deepest fear is that we are powerful beyond measure. It is our light, not our darkness that most frightens us."

Another reason why many resist the power of choice and the choice of power is that they do not believe it is theirs to wield. For example, I have noticed in my Baptist Christian tradition that there is a way of practicing the faith that vests God and God alone with power. Persons testify about "turning problems over to God" and witness to "waiting for God to move" in this or that manner. I do not mean to condemn this sentiment, especially when what is behind it is an abiding loyalty to God's sovereignty. But one need not abandon personal power out of respect for God. In Genesis 1:26, power or "dominion" is a gift that God gives humanity. Leaning into our power, our personal choice-making capacity, is one of the countless ways we show God gratitude.

The next time you turn something over to God or tell God to decide something for you, wait a moment. You may hear God say gently but firmly:

Deal with it. For my sake and yours, please deal with it. I am with you. I will help you, but dare to decide and live responsibly with the results of your choice. If I wanted to do it all by myself, I would not have created you in the first place, especially with all the abilities and gifts I have placed inside of you. Besides, I love to see you engaging challenges, creating possibilities, and choosing between options. I love watching you grow.

Notes

1. Frederick Buechner, *Listening to Your Life* (San Francisco: Harper, 1992), 234.
2. Anthony DeMello, *Awareness* (New York: Doubleday, 1990), 28.
3. Helmut Thielicke, *Notes from a Wayfarer* (New York: Paragon House, 1995), 418.
4. Coretta Scott King, *My Life with Martin Luther King Jr.* (New York: Holt, Rinehart and Winston, 1969), 15.
5. Judith Jamison, *Dancing Spirit* (New York: Anchor Books, 1993), 264.
6. Lucille Clifton, *Blessing the Boats* (Rochester, N.Y.: BOA Editions, 2000), 82.

Exercise

This space is reserved for your first Life Line Reflection. I will enjoy reading it. Please e-mail it to me at Kjones58@aol.com. With your permission I may publish it at www.savoringpace.com.

Along the Way

by Shari L. Smothers

Walking through my life hurriedly,
I saw thoughts flash by.
And in my rush to end my day
I went right by a gift for me.

Only in my bed did I
realize—that thing was a
blessing in the road.
I wanted it, so I hoped

I could go back and get it.
But the next day
when I went to see,
there was a man, standing

smiling because he got
the blessing meant for me.
I decided to slow down
for a week, to see

what I might find along my path
to bless me. I walked, slowly, more deliberately,
acknowledging people along the way,
feeling the breeze, watching the blowing leaves.

And at the close of the week
there was nothing I could find
along my path, that was a gift
to me. I sniffed the last flower,

and picked up the pace,
alright with having missed my gift.
After I was back to my schedule
for a month or so,

I looked back at that week
I searched my path for a blessing
and found not one thing.
I reflected on how nice that week was,

never minding. And the last
of the reflection came with tears.
The peaceful pace I had touched that week,
almost as though someone else received it,
was the stuff that was my treasure.

three tools to help you resist the rush and crush of life

Rest in the Storm: Self-Care Strategies for Clergy and Other Caregivers
Dr. Jones's first book has helped thousands of caregivers to understand that they are no less precious to God than the work they do or the people they serve. Noted author Dr. Richard Swenson states, "In writing that often reaches prose-poetry, Kirk Jones raises an urgent stop sign: Stop believing that chronic exhaustion is normal, that a listless spirit is inevitable, that burnout is piety…. Do your future a favor—buy this book and read it often."

Savoring Pace Life Lines
A collection of fifty cards featuring inspirational phrases that will help you change your living pace, one thought at a time. Pick a card in the morning to use as your theme for the day; carry extra cards with you to share with co-workers; include cards in mailings to friends. You will discover many different ways to live and share *Savoring Pace Life Lines*.

Weekly Savoring Pace Life Line Reflection

You can receive fresh encouragement for maintaining your new savoring pace each Monday morning at www.savoring-pace.com. Expect to see a brand new Life Line, words of reflection, and a pace practice suggestion that will offer you a way to put the new Life Line into practice that very day.

To order *Rest in the Storm* and *Savoring Pace Life Lines*, call Judson Press at 800-458-3766, or order online at www.judsonpress.com.

about the author

KIRK BYRON JONES, D. MIN., PH.D., WAS A PASTOR FOR twenty years. Presently a professor at Andover Newton Theological School, he serves as guest preacher and teacher at churches, schools, and conferences around the country.

Dr. Jones lives in Randolph, Massachusetts, with his wife, Bunnie, and their four children, Jasmine, Jared, Joya, and Jovonna.

For information regarding speaking engagements and workshops related to the subjects of his books, contact Dr. Jones at 781-961-1816 or kjones58@aol.com.